PREFACE

<u>Finding out about food</u> is designed as an introduction to the study of home economics for pupils aged nine to fourteen.

The book contains six chapters, each of which is divided into self-contained double-page units. Each unit ends with questions designed to reinforce understanding of the text.

The first five chapters include simple experiments and practical 'Things to do' which can be carried out within the home economics lesson, plus ideas for investigative homework. Each chapter ends with a section of 'Further work' including crosswords, quizzes, and fun things to do.

Chapter 6 contains a selection of recipes, which have been chosen to illustrate a range of cookery skills. Most of the dishes can be prepared and cooked within an hour-long home economics lesson, and they are easy to transport and to reheat when necessary.

It is hoped that this book will awaken pupils' interest in home economics, and encourage them to pursue the subject in more detail in later years.

Acknowledgements

Illustrations are by Ann Blockley, Jane Cradock-Watson, Sarah De'Ath, Marie-Hélène Jeeves, Kate Simunek and Shirley Anne Walker. Cover photograph by Roger Charlesson.

The publishers would like to thank the following for permission to reproduce photographs: Biophoto Associates 16, 53 (above), 88 (middle left and right); Birds Eye Wall's 94 (below), 95; British Meat 53 (below); Roger Charlesson 17, 30, 32, 33, 36, 39 (below), 41, 50 (above), 71, 88 (below left), 89, 95, 112; Dutch Dairy Bureau 51; Egg Information Bureau 38, 39 (above); Electrolux 81; Richard and Sally Greenhill 6, 10, 26 (above); Health Education Council 71; S. Heap 27 (below), 55 (below); H. J. Heinz Company 26 (below), 93 (above); Imperial War Museum 14; John Radcliffe Hospital Medical Illustration Department 15; Kellogg Company of Great Britain 69; La Leche League/Rosa Ibanez 27 (above), 28; Leybold–Heraeus 94 (above); Lyons Maid 47; Mansell Collection 43; Meat and Livestock Commission 52 (above); Milk Marketing Board 42, 46, 48 (left), 50 (below); Ministry of Agriculture 61; National Dairy Council 48 (right); Tony Neilson 57 (above); Proctor & Gamble 21; Sea Fish Industry Authority 56; St. Ivel 73 (below); Tesco 22, 57 (below); John Topham 7, 52 (middle and below), 55 (above); Tower Housewares 93 (below); Van den Berghs & Jurgens 73 (above); Vegetarian Society 30; Wall's Meat Company 54; C. James Webb 88 (above right), 91.

The pyramid on page 24 is from the Australian Nutrition Foundation.

The table of food values on page 29 is reproduced from 'The Composition of Foods' by R. A. McCance and E. M. Widdowson, by kind permission of Her Majesty's Stationery Office. Crown copyright.

Finding out about
FOOD

Jenny Ridgwell

Oxford University Press

Oxford University Press, Great Clarendon Street, Oxford OX2 6DP

Oxford New York
Auckland Bangkok Buenos Aires Cape Town Chennai
Dar es Salaam Delhi Hong Kong Istanbul Karachi Kolkata
Kuala Lumpur Madrid Melbourne Mexico City Mumbai Nairobi
São Paulo Shanghai Singapore Taipei Tokyo Toronto

with an associated company in Berlin

Oxford is a trademark of Oxford University Press

© Oxford University Press 1983

First published 1983
Reprinted 1983, 1984, 1985, 1986, 1987, 1988, 1990, 1991,
1993, 1994 (twice), 1996, 1997, 1998, 2000 (twice), 2002

ISBN 0 19 832716 1

Set by Wyvern Typesetting Ltd, Bristol
Printed in China

CONTENTS

1. NUTRITION

INTRODUCTION

Staying fit and healthy is fun. To keep fit and healthy you will need:
  1 good food   2 plenty of exercise   3 enough sleep.

Good food

In some countries in the world there is not enough food for everyone to eat. The people suffer from **malnutrition** (poor nourishment) and even **starvation** (no food at all).

In Britain there is enough food for everyone to be well fed and healthy, but some people still suffer from malnutrition because they eat the wrong foods. For example, if people eat too much sugar their teeth may decay. People who eat too much food may become overweight and ill.

More and more, snacks and take-away meals are replacing meals where the family used to sit down to eat together. Snack foods, sweets, and fizzy drinks fill you up, but provide few of the useful materials needed to keep the body fit and healthy. So, too many snacks and not enough 'proper food' can lead to poor health and malnutrition.

Although scientists now know a great deal about the value of food for health, many people still do not understand the importance of eating sensibly.

Here are some simple rules for eating well:

Too many fizzy drinks and sweet foods can make children overweight.

Good eating habits

1 Eat a wide variety of foods.
2 Avoid eating too much fat. Use less butter or margarine on bread, and cut down on fried food and cakes and biscuits.
3 Avoid too many sweet foods: sweets, fizzy drinks, biscuits, chocolates.
4 Eat plenty of fresh fruit and vegetables.
5 Eat more cereal foods, such as bread, rice, and breakfast cereals. Wholemeal bread is especially good.

Exercise

Exercise can be fun. More and more people are taking up jogging and joining sports centres. Exercise can be as simple as walking to school or work, or as energetic as football or disco dancing.

Exercise uses up energy which comes from the Calories in food (see page 12). The more energetic the exercise, the more Calories are used. For example, walking uses 270 Calories per hour, and tennis uses 355.

Because exercise increases the body's needs for energy, the blood must be pumped round the body quicker, to supply the muscles with extra food for energy.

Jogging helps you to keep fit.

Experiment to show how exercise increases the heart beat

You will need: a friend
a watch with a second hand

The normal pulse rate is seventy-two beats per minute. Find your pulse by placing your fingers on your neck, half-way between the ear and the mouth, and counting the beats for one minute.

Now exercise. *Either* run on the spot, *or* climb up and down on a chair, for six two-minute sessions. After each exercise session, count your pulse beat for one minute.

Ask your friend to time these exercise sessions and record the pulse rate. After the six exercise sessions, rest for ten minutes, then count the pulse rate for one minute.

Draw a graph to record your results. What was the effect of the exercise on your pulse rate, and what happened after a rest?

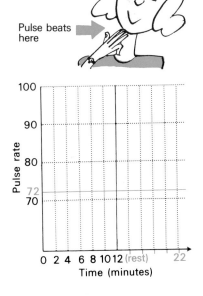

Pulse beats here

Pulse rate

100
90
80
72
70

0 2 4 6 8 10 12 (rest) 22
Time (minutes)

Rest and sleep

Few things are more important than a good night's sleep, as sleep rests the body and gives it time to repair worn-out tissues. Lack of sleep causes tiredness and dullness during the day. On average, adults need eight hours' sleep a night, and young people need quite a lot more.

Questions
1 How can poor eating habits damage our health?
2 Use the rules for good eating habits to plan your meals for one day.

Homework
Make a colourful poster with the title: 'How to stay healthy'.

7

'It's a very odd thing, as odd as can be, that whatever Miss T eats, turns into Miss T.' (*Walter de la Mare*)

There are three main reasons why the body needs food:
1 for **growth and repair**
2 for **energy and warmth**
3 for **protection.**
   The materials found in food help to build and repair the body. They provide the body with energy and help it keep warm. They help the body to remain healthy.
   The materials found in food are called **nutrients**. It is important to know which foods contain which nutrients, and what job each nutrient does, so that we can choose the right foods to keep us healthy.
   The food we choose to eat each day (whatever the choice!) is known as our **diet.**

Growth and repair

Our life begins as an egg, about the size of a pinhead. Over the years, the nutrients from body-building foods provide the body with the materials needed to build new cells. Millions of these cells, which can only be seen under a microscope, make up the different parts of the body, such as skin, muscle, and bones. Once the body is fully grown, body-building foods are still necessary to repair and replace worn-out cells.

The names of the nutrients needed for growth and repair are:

Protein   Minerals   Vitamins

Energy and body warmth

For twenty-four hours a day, the body needs energy from food. Energy helps the body to move, breathe, and even read and sleep. The more we move, the more energy we require.
   Human beings are warm-blooded animals, with a body temperature of 37°C. Energy from food maintains this temperature and keeps us warm.

The names of the nutrients needed for energy and body warmth are:

Carbohydrate   Fat   Protein

Protection

The body needs to keep fit and healthy. Certain nutrients help-to protect us against illness, and keep the body in good working order.

The names of these nutrients are:

| Vitamins   Minerals |

Vitamins and minerals are only required in small amounts, but they are still vital to our health.

Summary

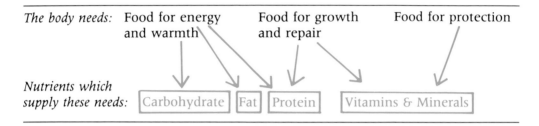

The body needs: Food for energy and warmth   Food for growth and repair   Food for protection

Nutrients which supply these needs: Carbohydrate   Fat   Protein   Vitamins & Minerals

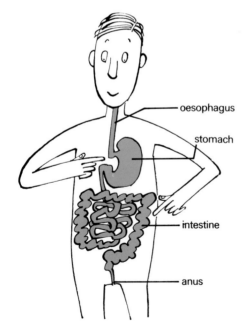

oesophagus

stomach

intestine

anus

What happens when food is eaten?

When food is eaten, it is broken down, and changed into small particles which can be absorbed into the body cells. This process is called **digestion**.

Digestion begins in the **mouth** where food is **chewed** and **mixed** with **saliva** (spit). The food is swallowed and passes down the **oesophagus** into a bag called the **stomach**. The stomach churns and squeezes the food before passing it into the **intestine**.

Different digestive juices work on the food, breaking it into particles which are small enough to pass through the intestine wall, into the **blood stream**, and on into the **body cells**. When the food has reached the end of the intestine, most nutrients and water have been removed, and the waste matter is passed out through the **anus**.

Questions
1 What are nutrients? Which nutrients provide the body with the materials for (a) growth and repair, (b) energy, (c) protection?
2 What is a 'diet'?
3 Why does the body need to digest food?

Homework
Write down all the items of food and drink which made up your diet yesterday.

The five groups of nutrients are:
Protein Carbohydrate Fat Vitamins Minerals

Nearly all foods contain more than one nutrient. There are just a few exceptions to this, such as sugar (carbohydrate only), and some cooking oils (fat only). A healthy diet is one which includes foods containing nutrients from each of the five groups, so it is important to know which foods are good sources of which nutrients.

Protein

The word protein comes from the Greek word meaning 'I am first'. It is the first and most important nutrient in our diet, and we cannot live without it. In Britain we are not likely to be short of protein.

Why do we need protein?

All living things, both plants and animals, need protein to grow.

Children are still growing, and need protein to build up the millions of body cells which form muscles, skin, nerves, and body organs. Although adults have stopped growing, they still need protein to replace and renew worn-out or damaged body cells. When the skin is cut, new cells must be formed to heal the wound.

If more protein is eaten than the body needs for growth and repair, the spare protein is broken down and used for energy. This can be wasteful, as protein-rich foods are expensive.

Protein helps children to grow.

The body needs protein to repair any damage.

Summary

Protein is necessary for →
- growth of cells
- repair and replacement of old and damaged cells
- energy from spare protein

Which foods are rich in protein?

Protein is found in all living things, plants and animals. Some foods are better sources of protein than others.

Animal foods which are good sources of protein include meat, fish, cheese, eggs, and milk.

Vegetable foods which are good sources of protein include the seeds of plants – peas, beans, cereals, nuts, and rice.

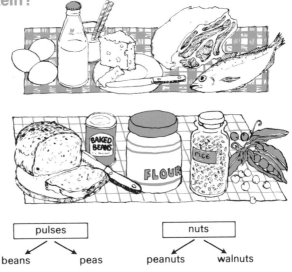

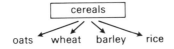

cereals	pulses	nuts
oats wheat barley rice	beans peas	peanuts walnuts

Animal protein foods are usually more expensive than vegetable protein foods. A sensible diet includes a mixture of animal and vegetable foods, e.g. bread and cheese, breakfast cereal and milk, egg and chips.

TVP

Soya beans are rich in protein. Recently, soya beans have been used to manufacture a food which looks and tastes like meat, called **textured vegetable protein** (TVP).

TVP is made by squeezing out soya-flour dough through a nozzle. This makes a spongy mass, which is then coloured and flavoured to resemble meat. TVP is dried, so that when water is added, it can be used in savoury dishes such as mince or sausages.

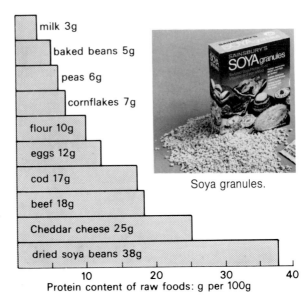

milk 3g
baked beans 5g
peas 6g
cornflakes 7g
flour 10g
eggs 12g
cod 17g
beef 18g
Cheddar cheese 25g
dried soya beans 38g

10   20   30   40
Protein content of raw foods: g per 100g

Soya granules.

Questions

1 Name *three* good sources of animal protein and *three* good sources of vegetable protein. Suggest *four* ways of serving animal and vegetable protein foods together in meals.
2 Why is protein important in the diet?

Homework

Protein-rich foods can be expensive. Find out the cost per kilo of the following foods: (a) pigs' liver, (b) stewing beef, (c) Cheddar cheese, (d) cod, (e) frozen peas, (f) white flour.

Plan a hot meal to include two of these foods.

CARBOHYDRATES AND FATS

Carbohydrates and fats are energy-giving nutrients. Spare protein not needed for growth or repair can also be broken down and used for energy.

Energy is needed for activity, but even when we are resting, we need energy. For example, the body needs energy to remain warm, for the heart to pump blood around the body, and for the lungs to take in air.

The energy value of foods is measured in a unit of heat called the **calorie**. Because this unit is so small, when talking about food we use the term **Calorie** or **kilocalorie** (1000 calories).

Fat contains twice as many Calories as carbohydrates or protein.

1 g fat = 9 kcal
1 g protein or carbohydrate = 4 kcal

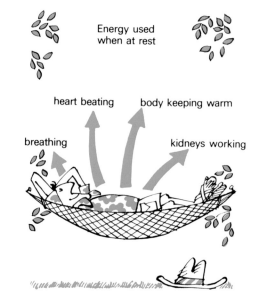

Energy used when at rest

heart beating   body keeping warm

breathing   kidneys working

Carbohydrates

Carbohydrates are made by plants from **carbon dioxide** and **water**. This process is called **photosynthesis** and uses energy from the sun. See p. 58.

Groups of carbohydrates include:

sugars
starches
substances like cellulose

Examples of **sugars** are:
    table sugar, natural sugars found in fruit and milk.

Examples of **starches** are:
    flour, bread, potatoes, root vegetables, rice, beans, peas, yams.

Examples of foods containing **cellulose** are:
    fruits, vegetables.

After digestion, carbohydrates are converted into **glucose**, a simple sugar. This glucose is passed to all parts of the body for use as energy.

If people eat more carbohydrate than they use as energy, the spare carbohydrate is stored in the body as fat.

To do: The saliva (spit) in the mouth begins to change starch into a sugar called maltose. Slowly chew a piece of dry bread, which contains starch, and notice how the bread gradually tastes sweeter due to the formation of maltose.

Fats

Fats are a more concentrated source of energy than carbohydrates.

Fat can be found as:

Animal fat: butter, lard, meat, milk, cream, oily fish, cheese.

Vegetable fat: nuts and seeds, such as peas, beans, cereals.

Margarine and cooking oils can be made from animal and vegetable fats. Oils are simply fats which are liquid at room temperature.

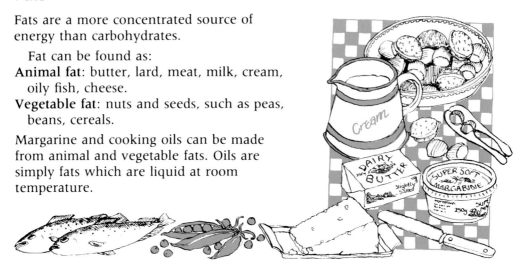

Fat has other uses:

1 Body fat is stored under the skin, and helps keep the body warm.
2 Fats contain vitamins A and D.
3 Fat makes some dry foods easier to eat, e.g. butter on bread, margarine in mashed potatoes.
4 Some methods of cooking, such as frying and roasting, require fat.

Fat and heart disease

Researchers have discovered that fats affect the amount of a substance in the blood called **cholesterol**. It is thought that a build-up of cholesterol in the blood may be one cause of heart disease.

The researchers suggest that less fat should be eaten in the diet. It is easy to cut down on the amount of fat eaten. For example, spread less butter on bread, grill food instead of frying it, and cut fat off meat.

Questions

1 Name three foods rich in fat and three foods rich in carbohydrates.
2 How does the body use carbohydrates and fats?
3 Suggest *five* ways to cut down on the amount of fat eaten.

Homework

Collect pictures of foods and arrange them under these group headings: **sugary foods**, **starchy foods**, **fatty foods**. Some examples may belong to two or three groups. 13

The word 'vitamin' comes from the word 'vital', which means essential for life. Vitamins are chemicals found in food which are necessary to keep the body healthy. Vitamins were not discovered until the beginning of this century, although for hundreds of years people knew that certain foods would cure certain diseases.

As scientists discovered the different vitamins, they named them after the letters in the alphabet. The most important vitamins are A, B, C, and D. Each vitamin has a different chemical name and a different function.

Vitamin A

This was the first vitamin to be named in 1916. Vitamin A is found in fats, dairy produce, and oily fish. It is also found in green and orange vegetables in the form of **carotene**. This carotene is converted by the body into vitamin A.

During the food rationing of the Second World War, when butter was in short supply, people were encouraged to get vitamin A from carrots, by a character called Dr Carrot.

Name of the vitamin	What the vitamin does	Foods rich in the vitamin
A (Chemical name: retinol)	Necessary for growth, healthy skin and eyes.	Dairy foods, margarine, eggs, oily fish, green and orange fruit and vegetables.

B Vitamins

There are at least *eleven* B vitamins, but the three important ones are **thiamin, riboflavin,** and **nicotinic acid**. These vitamins dissolve in water.

As long ago as 1897, a scientist noticed that chickens fed on left-over polished white rice became ill. When these same chickens were given husks (outsides) of the rice, they got better. Today we know that rice husks contain thiamin which will cure this illness.

In Britain, the thiamin-rich wheat husk is removed to make white flour. Since thiamin is important in our diet, a law was made to put the thiamin back into white flour.

Name of the vitamins	What the vitamins do	Foods rich in the vitamins
B (Chemical names: thiamin, riboflavin, nicotinic acid)	Help the body obtain energy from food. Necessary for good health.	Liver, kidney, flour, bread, meat, potatoes.

Vitamin C

Vitamin C dissolves in water, and is found in fresh fruit and vegetables.

In the 17th century, British sailors carried lemons and limes on board ship to prevent the crew from dying of a disease called scurvy. This earned the sailors the nickname 'limeys', a word still used today! Later, scientists discovered that citrus fruits contained valuable vitamin C.

Vitamin C is easily lost during the preparation and cooking of fruit and vegetables. (See p. 60.)

Name of the vitamin	What the vitamin does	Foods rich in the vitamin
C (Chemical name: ascorbic acid)	Keeps the skin, bones, and muscles healthy. Increases resistance to infection, and helps the body absorb iron.	Green vegetables, fruit, especially citrus fruits, potatoes, rosehip syrup.

Vitamin D

Because vitamin D is only found in a few foods, it is added to margarine and to some baby foods.

The disease called **rickets** is caused by lack of vitamin D and calcium. It is found in children who eat a poor diet, and who rarely play in the sunshine. Their bones become so weak that their legs bend under the weight of their body. Rickets was once so common that it was called the 'English disease'. In spite of better food and vitamin drops and pills, some children still suffer from rickets in this country.

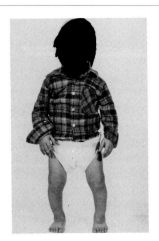

A child with rickets.

Name of the vitamin	What the vitamin does	Foods rich in the vitamin
D (Chemical name: cholecalciferol)	Needed to form strong bones and teeth. Prevents rickets and helps the body absorb calcium.	Added to margarine; found in butter, milk, eggs, oily fish. The action of sunlight on the skin also forms vitamin D in the body.

Questions
1 Describe what four different vitamins do, and name two foods rich in each vitamin.
2 Which vitamins dissolve in water and which dissolve in fat?

Homework
Look at the labels on the following foods and make a list of the vitamins which are added: (a) instant potato, (b) margarine, (c) baby food, (d) breakfast cereals. Why do you think these foods have added vitamins?

There are about fifteen important minerals which can be obtained from food. Minerals have three main functions:

1 To help form bones and teeth – calcium, phosphorus, fluorine.
2 To form body fluids – sodium, chlorine, potassium.
3 To make up body cells, such as muscles, liver, and blood – iron, sulphur, phosphorus.

A well-balanced diet will supply enough of all these minerals. Extra amounts are only needed in special cases; for example, pregnant women and growing children may need increased supplies of calcium or iron.

Calcium

1 Calcium, with phosphorus, is essential to help form strong bones and teeth.
2 Calcium helps the blood clot properly.
3 Calcium is essential for muscles and nerves to work properly.

Children, pregnant women and breast-feeding mothers need extra calcium for growing bones. Too little calcium results in stunted growth and even rickets, in children.

Milk and cheese are rich sources of calcium. By law, white flour and bread are enriched with chalk (calcium carbonate).

Vitamin D helps calcium be absorbed into the body. Foods rich in calcium and vitamin D can be eaten together, for example:
   white bread and margarine
   sardines on toast
   egg and bacon pie
   cauliflower in cheese sauce.

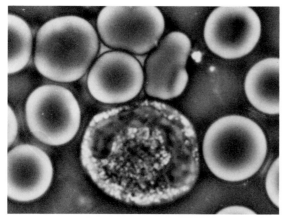

Red blood cells magnified 2000 times. The large cell is a white blood cell.

Iron

The adult body contains about 4 g of iron, enough to make a large nail! Iron is needed to form part of a substance called **haemoglobin**, which gives red blood cells their colour. The red blood cells carry oxygen from the lungs to all body tissues to provide the tissues with energy. Red blood cells last about 120 days, and when they break down, their iron is saved and used for new cells.

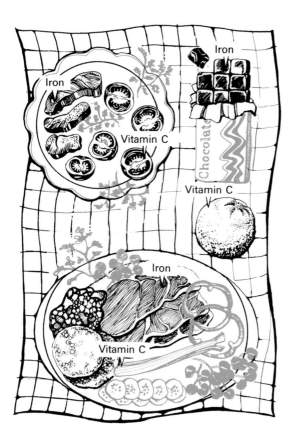

When blood is lost from the body, valuable iron is lost as well. Women lose blood every month during their periods, and blood can be lost from cuts and wounds. This lost iron must be replaced, otherwise iron-deficiency **anaemia** could result. A person suffering from anaemia may look pale, and feel tired and weak.

Rich sources of iron include liver, kidney, meat, chocolate, and white bread and flour which are enriched with iron. In Britain, one third of our iron comes from cereals, especially bread, one third from meat, and the rest from vegetables and other sources.

Serving foods rich in iron and vitamin C together, e.g. liver and tomatoes, meat salad, chocolate and orange, helps the body to make better use of the iron.

Fluorine

This mineral helps prevent tooth decay, especially in young children. Fluorine is added to water supplies in some parts of Britain, and fluoride toothpaste is a useful source of this mineral.

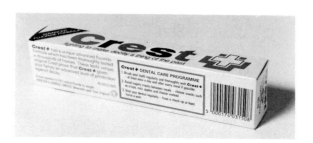

Questions

1 Name **two** important mineral salts, and describe why they are important in the diet. Which foods supply these minerals?
2 Which minerals are needed for healthy teeth?

Homework

1 Plan a day's meals for a pregnant woman, to include foods rich in calcium and iron.
2 Visit a chemist's shop and make a list of:
   (a) tablets or 'tonics' rich in iron,
   (b) types of fluoride toothpaste.
   What claims, if any, do these products make?

Dietary fibre

Our ancestors were used to eating foods that contained plenty of dietary fibre: cereals such as wheat and oats, seed vegetables such as beans and peas, and fruits and nuts.

Our diets today contain much less dietary fibre. Foods such as eggs, meat, and fish contain no fibre at all, and 'refined' foods such as white bread and polished rice contain much less dietary fibre than the wholegrain foods, such as wholemeal flour and brown rice.

Why is dietary fibre important?

Dietary fibre cannot be broken down in the digestive system, so it passes through the intestine, absorbing water, and increasing in bulk. This bulk helps the muscles of the intestine to push undigested food out of the body.

If the diet contains little fibre, then there is less bulk to stimulate the muscles of the intestine, and the undigested food becomes a hard mass which is difficult, and sometimes painful, for the body to get rid of. This problem is known as constipation. People who eat enough dietary fibre should not suffer from constipation.

How much dietary fibre is there in different foods?

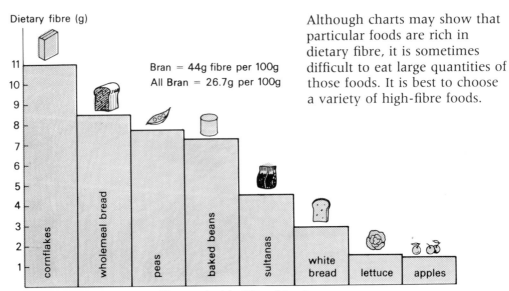

Dietary fibre (g)

Bran = 44g fibre per 100g
All Bran = 26.7g per 100g

Fibre content in 100g of food

Although charts may show that particular foods are rich in dietary fibre, it is sometimes difficult to eat large quantities of those foods. It is best to choose a variety of high-fibre foods.

To do: Choose five foods from the chart, including wholemeal bread and bran. Weigh out 50 g of each food and decide which food you could eat the most of.

How to eat more dietary fibre

1 Eat more bread, especially wholemeal bread.
2 Eat cereals for breakfast, especially wholegrain cereals and those containing bran.
3 Use more seed vegetables in cooking – peas, beans, and lentils.
4 Replace refined foods with wholegrain products such as wholewheat pasta, brown rice, wholemeal flour.
5 Eat plenty of fresh fruit and vegetables. Eat skins of apples and pears, and cook potatoes in their skins.

To do: Select some tempting recipes containing white flour. Try out these recipes, replacing half of the white flour with wholemeal flour.

Water

Our body contains about 45 litres of water. We might live for over two months without food, but we can exist for only three or four days without drinking.

Every tissue and organ of the body contains water. Water is necessary for digestion to take place. It is needed to help wash away waste products in the form of urine, and water is a necessary part of sweat, which helps keep the body cool.

We need to drink a litre of water or other liquid a day. We can also get about 0.8 litres of water a day from food. The chart opposite shows the water content of some foods.

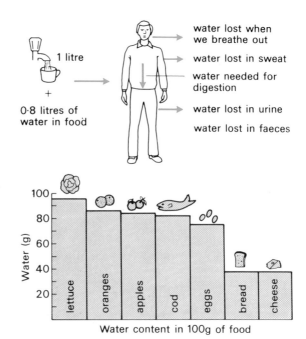

Water content in 100g of food

Questions

1 Why is dietary fibre important in the diet? Name three good sources of dietary fibre.
2 An elderly lady suffers from constipation. Plan a day's meals containing good sources of dietary fibre, which might help her with her problem.
3 Give three examples of foods with a high water content.

Homework

1 Visit your local supermarket and make a list of:
   (a) The different wholegrain products for sale, e.g. pasta, rice, bread.
   (b) Bran-enriched foods, e.g. breakfast cereals.
   (c) Types of brown and wholemeal bread sold.
2 Describe **three** recipes which include wholemeal flour or added bran. Illustrate the recipes with drawings.

19

The road to health

How well do you look after yourself? Start out on the road to health with ten points, and see how you shape up.

1 If you start the day with a proper breakfast and not just a cup of tea, score two points.

2 If you brush your teeth twice a day, score two points.

3 At mid-morning break, do you usually eat sweets or biscuits? If so, lose two points.

6 If you skip lunch and eat chips or crisps instead, lose two points.

5 If you eat either fresh fruit or vegetables every day, score two points.

4 If you eat some bread and potatoes every day, score two points.

7 If you regularly eat wholemeal or brown bread, score two points.

8 If you are still slimming after the doctor says you are the correct weight, lose two points.

9 If you are more than four kilos overweight, lose two points.

12 If you have just started to smoke, or smoke regularly, lose four points.

11 If you take regular exercise by walking to school or taking part in a sport, score four points.

10 If you visit the dentist regularly every six months, score two points.

How did you score?

26–22	20–18	Below 18
Well done. You know how to look after yourself.	With just a few changes, you could be on the right road to health.	Poor. You need to think about eating different foods and looking after yourself better.

Experiments

Starch test

Iodine can be used to detect the presence of starch in food, but remember that iodine is poisonous. It is dangerous to conduct this experiment in an area where food is prepared.

Using a pipette, put a few drops of iodine on to a selection of foods. Iodine will change from reddish-brown to blue-black if starch is present. Test potatoes, bread, rice, etc.

Fat test

Fat can be detected by rubbing a piece of food on to a brown paper bag. The fat will leave a greasy mark which lets light through. If the food is wet, allow time for a water mark to dry out. Test cheese, biscuits, bread, margarine, etc.

Bran test

Bran is the indigestible outside husk of wheat and other grains. During digestion, bran absorbs water and swells, forming a bulky mass which helps food to move through the digestive system.

Find out how much water dry bran can absorb. Place a tablespoonful of bran in a bowl. Add water, a teaspoonful at a time, and count how many spoonfuls are needed to form a moist mass.

What happens if you keep adding water?

Plaque test

This experiment will help you to find out the best way to clean your teeth.

Plaque is a sticky white substance which contains millions of bacteria. Plaque lives off food in the mouth, and grows on the surface of the teeth. Bacteria in the plaque produce an acid which attacks tooth enamel and causes decay. Plaque produces poisons which can damage gums and lead to tooth loss.

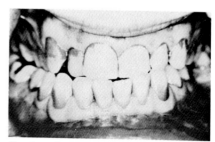

Teeth stained by plaque-disclosing tablets.

For this experiment you will need some **plaque-disclosing tablets** which you can buy from a chemist's.

1 Slowly chew the disclosing tablet, moving it around the mouth.
2 Rinse out the mouth with water. Look in a mirror. The areas of plaque will be stained red.
3 Brush the teeth with a sideways movement. Rinse out the mouth and notice areas where plaque remains.
4 Now brush the teeth with a downwards movement, rinse, and brush again until all areas of stain are removed.

The time spent brushing the teeth to remove the red stain is the normal time which should be spent on cleaning your teeth.

2. PLANNING MEALS

SHOPPING

'England is a nation of shopkeepers.' (*Napoleon*)

The history of shopping

In the Middle Ages, people grew their own food, or bought it from country markets or shops in the town. As towns grew larger, the number of grocery shops increased. In those days, grocers had to weigh and pack up each item separately, and customers waited a long time to be served. Shop assistants often worked a fifteen-hour day, finishing at ten or eleven o'clock at night, and they could be sacked if they displeased the customers.

The supermarket was first started in America in 1919, by a man called Clarence Saunders. He decided to weigh and pack his goods, place them on shelves, and let his customers help themselves. His idea was such a success that it has been copied all over the world! Supermarkets were introduced into Britain in the 1950s and since then, shops have become larger, brighter, and cleaner places to shop in.

Shopping in the future

As more and more people use their cars when they go out shopping, parking is becoming a problem. Large under-cover shopping centres or **hypermarkets** are being built on the outskirts of towns, with plenty of car parking space. Everything can be bought from these centres – from food and clothes to furniture and electrical goods.

In modern supermarkets, shoppers can choose their own fruit and vegetables and hand them to the assistant to weigh.

Shopping for food

By planning ahead and making a shopping list, nourishing meals for the week can be chosen without overspending.

Special offers and price reductions can be very tempting when shopping. Decide first whether you really need the food, and then whether it is good value for money.

Different types of shop

Corner shops usually sell only a small range of goods, and prices may be high because of the long hours that the shop stays open, and the small turnover of goods. These shops are useful when buying a few items, or for emergencies. They are often closer to home than large supermarkets.

Supermarkets must have over 2000 square feet of floor space and three or more tills. They sell a wide variety of foods and prices are often lower, because there is a large turnover of goods. Most food and household goods can be purchased from one shop.

Specialist shops such as butchers', bakers', fishmongers' and greengrocers' usually sell only one type of food. The shop assistants can give you advice when you buy food. Specialist shops are still popular. 62% of fresh meat is bought from butchers', and 48% of fresh vegetables from greengrocers'.

Street markets sell low-priced goods, because the trader has only to rent the stall for that day. Fruit and vegetables are usually very fresh, but all purchases should be carefully checked.

Cleanliness in shops

1 Shop in *clean* food shops. Avoid shops where the shop assistants have poor standards of hygiene, such as touching food with dirty hands or smoking when handling food.
2 Dogs and cats should not be allowed in food shops.
3 Food should be properly stored. Food such as meat, fish, and dairy products must be kept cool.

Questions

1 Write down the advantages and disadvantages of shopping in the following places: (a) corner shops, (b) supermarkets, (c) specialist shops, (d) street markets. Give reasons why you think many people prefer to shop in supermarkets.
2 Make a list of rules to encourage shop assistants to keep good standards of hygiene.

Homework

1 Write a report comparing two of your local food shops. Assess each shop for: helpfulness, good service, cleanliness, clearly priced goods, and the condition of the shop (whether it is well decorated, noisy, too warm, etc.).
2 Manufacturers package goods to attract buyers. Show how different foods have been made to look tempting and interesting. Use labels, pictures, and advertisements to illustrate your work.

There is no one magic food which contains all the nutrients that we need for a healthy diet. No food is especially 'good' or 'bad' for us. However, sometimes if we eat too much or too little of certain foods, we have an unhealthy diet. For example, too many sweets can lead to tooth decay, and too little food can cause loss of weight and **malnutrition**. One simple rule for eating healthily is to eat a variety of foods – different fruits, vegetables, snack foods and breakfast cereals. A second rule is not to eat too much of anything, especially foods rich in fat, sugar and alcohol.

You could use the **Healthy Diet Pyramid** to help choose a variety of foods that you need for a healthy diet.

Healthy diet pyramid

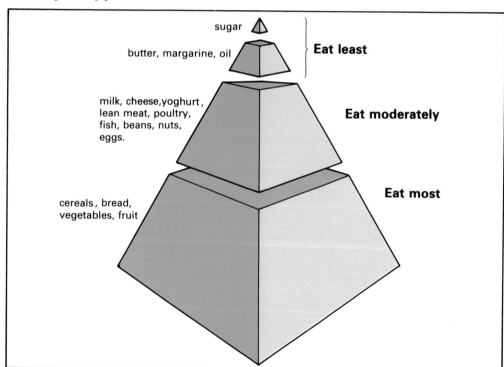

Eat most: cereals, bread, vegetables, fruit
What does this mean? For many people, a better diet could simply mean eating more bread, pasta, rice, fruits and vegetables. These foods help to increase the dietary fibre in our diet as well as providing vitamin C and minerals.

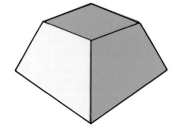

Eat moderately: milk, cheese, yoghurt, lean meat

All these foods contain a variety of nutrients, especially protein needed for body building. However, some, such as cheese, contain nearly one-third fat. So these foods must be eaten in moderation – a little of each at one time.

Eat least: butter, margarine, oil, sugar

Heart disease has been linked with eating fatty food. In the U.K. the figures for early death from heart disease are amongst the highest in the world. So, cut down on thickly-spread butter! Sugar is linked with tooth decay, so we should cut down on sweets, biscuits and sugary foods. Health experts have suggested that as well as eating a variety of foods we should:

1 eat more bread, cereals and starchy foods
2 cut down on fat, especially *saturated fat* from animal foods
3 eat less sugary food
4 eat less salty food
5 drink less alcohol such as spirits and beer.

Healthy eating should be fun. A wide variety of foods is now available all year – salad foods are imported all year round, several varieties of canned beans are sold and many foods are frozen, ready for use. Food should be enjoyable. There is no point sitting down to a plate of 'healthy foods' if you won't eat it! You need not work out the nutrients for every meal – the body can store spare nutrients from previous meals to make up for missed lunches and packets of sweets now and then.

Questions

1 Write a paragraph to describe what you think is meant by 'healthy eating'.
2 Make a list of all the food you ate yesterday. Draw up a table like the one below and fill in the foods you ate, under each heading. One example has been completed.

Foods to eat most of	Foods to eat moderately	Foods to eat least of
cereals, fruits	milk, eggs, cheese, meat	fats, sugar
cornflakes orange juice toast	milk with cornflakes	sugar with cornflakes
		butter with toast marmalade with toast
	tea with milk	tea with sugar

Homework

Keep a food diary for three days. Write down the variety of different foods that you eat. Use these headings and add more of your own
Headings: fruits, vegetables, drinks, snacks, cereals . . .
Did you have a variety of each? Could you change your diet?

Why people have different food needs

As we grow and develop, the way we lead our lives changes, and so our need for food changes. Scientists can calculate the amount of food we each need to eat. Results depend upon height, weight, age, whether a person is male or female, and how active he or she is. For example, large people may need more food than small people; older people need less energy-rich food than younger adults; active people need more food than those who take little exercise.

Babies and toddlers

During the first few months of life, human milk, or a special dried milk mix for babies, supplies nearly all the baby's needs. Fruit juice and multi-vitamin drops provide extra important vitamins.

When the baby is three to four months old, other foods should be added to the diet, because milk no longer supplies all the baby's needs. It is necessary to include foods which are a good source of iron, such as minced liver or white bread.

Human milk is the perfect food for babies.

Older babies can eat the same food as the rest of the family, but the food needs to be minced or strained and should not be too spicy or salty.

Sometimes children refuse to eat certain foods. Other foods containing similar nutrients should replace this food, e.g. vegetables can be replaced by fruit. The food could be disguised in other food, e.g. eggs added to puddings or mashed potato.

Older babies try a variety of foods.

Menu for a toddler

Breakfast	Lunch	Evening meal
Cereal with milk	Cottage cheese	Fish fingers,
Boiled egg,	sandwich	baked beans,
soldiers of toast	Fruit yoghurt	mashed potato
Milk	Orange juice	Stewed apple,
		custard
		Milk

Children

Children grow fast and are very active. In proportion to their body size, they need more nutrients than adults. Good sources of body-building foods include eggs, fish, meat, milk, and cheese. Calcium for bone growth can be obtained from white bread, cheese, and milk. Children should be encouraged to try different foods, so that they eat a varied and balanced diet. Too many sweets and starchy snacks can form bad eating habits, which may lead to tooth decay and overweight in later life.

Children should have a varied diet.

Teenagers

Teenagers usually need to eat more food than any other group because they are still growing and remain very active. Their large appetites are a sign that their bodies require extra food for the 'growth spurt' which takes place between the ages of twelve and nineteen. Body-building and protective foods are important for growth and fitness. Energy-giving foods are needed too. Girls should eat iron-rich foods such as meat, liver, and green vegetables, because they lose iron in blood during their periods.

Teenage girls need iron-rich foods.

Menu for an active teenager

Breakfast	Lunch	Evening meal
Cereal with milk	Cheeseburger,	Spaghetti
Boiled egg	chips, salad	bolognese
Toast, butter,	Orange	Apple pie and
marmalade	Chocolate bar,	custard
Tea	milk	Tea

Questions
1 Why do people need different amounts of food?
2 Why is it important for (a) children and (b) teenagers to eat a well-balanced diet?
3 Some children are 'fussy' eaters. Suggest how food can be made to look more interesting to encourage a young child to eat it.

Homework
1 Imagine that you had to plan a week's school lunches for some ten-year-olds. Give five different meals for the week.
2 Plan three meals which a nine-month-old baby might eat. What preparation is necessary so that the baby can eat the food easily?

Pregnancy and breast-feeding

During pregnancy, a woman needs to eat body-building and protective foods to help build the body of her baby, and keep them both fit and well. For the baby, foods rich in calcium and iron are needed to build bones and blood. Many pregnant women take tablets containing iron as well. During pregnancy, useful, nutritious foods include milk, eggs, bread, fish, and meat as well as fruit and vegetables.

A mother who is breast-feeding her baby needs to produce nourishing milk. She must eat food rich in protein, vitamins, and minerals in order to make this milk and remain healthy herself. If she eats a poorly balanced diet, her body will use up its stored nutrients to make milk and she will suffer.

A pregnant woman needs a well-balanced diet.

Elderly people

Older people tend to take less exercise than younger adults, and so they need to eat less energy-rich foods such as fats and sugars. However, older people still need the same amounts of vitamins, minerals, and proteins as young adults. Foods rich in dietary fibre, such as wholemeal bread, help to prevent constipation.

People living alone sometimes cannot be bothered to cook for themselves. Eggs, bread, and fresh fruit can provide nourishing and easy-to-prepare meals. Convenience foods also provide easily-prepared meals when shopping or cooking are difficult. Frozen fruit and vegetables can provide as much useful vitamin C as the fresh food.

Menu for an elderly person

	Breakfast	Lunch	Evening meal
	Bran-enriched cereal with milk	Ham and tomato sandwich	Fish pie, peas, potatoes
	Scrambled egg on toast	Banana	Baked apple and custard
	Tea	Tea	Tea

Slimmers

Many people are overweight because they eat too much and exercise too little. Energy-rich foods containing fat and carbohydrate are needed to keep the body active. However, if more of this food is eaten than the body needs, then the extra food is stored as body fat, and the person puts on weight. More than one third of the adults in this country are overweight, but very few children are fat. Children and teenagers should seek advice if they feel they need to lose weight. A serious illness called **anorexia nervosa** may be caused by over-enthusiastic slimming.

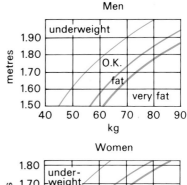

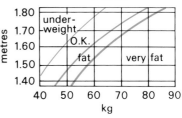

How to slim

To lose weight, the body must use up its excess store of fat. By eating less energy-rich food and taking more exercise, the body begins to use these reserves.

Some people try to lose weight quickly by drastically cutting down on the amount of food that they eat. This is known as 'crash dieting'. The person loses weight, but does not learn new eating habits, so they often return to their 'fat' way of eating.

Calorie counting is a popular way to slim because any food can be eaten within the chosen limit. An average adult woman needs a daily allowance of 1000–1200 Calories, and an average man 1500–1800 Calories, in order to lose weight. The slimming diet must be well balanced if the slimmer is to stay healthy.

Food	Calories per 25g
Bread, white	69
Bread, brown	68
All Bran	88
Cornflakes	104
Butter	226
Margarine	226
Cod, steamed	23
Apples, baked with skin	9
Apples, English, eating, fresh	13
Chicken, roast	54
Chocolate, plain	155
Sugar, white	112
Beans, baked	26

Calorie charts list the number of Calories in different foods.

Menu for a woman trying to slim

Breakfast	Lunch	Evening meal
Orange juice	Ham salad	Roast chicken, baked
Boiled egg	Bread and	potato, cabbage and
Toast and butter	butter	carrots
Tea with skimmed	Pear	Low-fat yoghurt
milk	Coffee	Coffee

Questions

1 Why must a pregnant woman eat nutritious food? Plan her meals for one day.
2 Why might elderly people find it difficult to cook for themselves?
3 Why do people become overweight and how can this extra weight be lost?
4 How can a Calorie-controlled diet help you lose weight?

Homework

Find out the names and costs of ten 'slimming products' found in the shops.

Invalids

For some illnesses, such as **anaemia** or **diabetes**, special diets are needed, and the doctor prescribes what the patient should eat.

Invalids generally require less energy-rich food because they are normally resting and not very active. Foods rich in protein, minerals, and vitamins, especially vitamin C, are essential to help them get better and repair any damages.

Invalids may not feel hungry, so they should be tempted with nourishing milk and fruit drinks. Food should be light and easy to digest, and fried or greasy food such as fish and chips should be avoided.

Suitable foods include milk drinks, puddings and sauces, raw and cooked fruit, and poached fish and egg dishes.

Menu for an invalid in bed recovering from flu

Breakfast	Lunch	Evening meal
Fruit juice	Cottage cheese	Fish in white
Poached egg on	salad	sauce, peas,
toast	Wholemeal bread	carrots
Tea	and butter	Lemon mousse
	Banana custard	Coffee
	Tea	

Vegetarians

Vegetarians do not eat animal flesh, and might not eat any animal products. People often choose to become vegetarians because they do not believe in killing animals for food. Some religions forbid the eating of animal food. Other people feel that it is wasteful to use valuable land to raise animals for meat. They think that the land should be used to produce more crops so that more people in the world could be fed.

There are three main types of vegetarian:

1 **Ovo-lacto-vegetarians** eat milk, eggs, and animal products, but not meat or fish.

2 **Lacto-vegetarians**, such as strict Hindus, avoid meat, fish, and eggs, but eat milk and cheese.

3 **Vegans** are the strictest vegetarians, who eat no animal food at all.

The Vegetarian Society produces leaflets to explain the reasons for becoming a vegetarian.

Meal planning for vegetarians

Vegetarians who eat eggs, milk, and cheese have no problems in balancing their diet, for these foods contain the same quality protein as meat and are rich in other nutrients.

Vegans need to plan their diets carefully since they are not able to eat any animal protein. A wide selection of beans, peas, nuts and cereals help to provide sufficient protein.

Seed foods tend to be bulky, and have little flavour, so interesting recipes should be chosen to make food tasty. Vegetables with good flavour and colour can liven up cereal and bean dishes. Peppers, tomatoes, onions, and parsley all add colour and flavour.

Menu for a vegan

	Breakfast	Lunch	Evening meal
	Muesli and apple	Vegetable curry,	Lentil rissoles,
	Toast, margarine,	rice	tomato sauce,
	marmalade	Orange	spaghetti, salad
	Tea	Coffee	Fruit in pastry flan

The soya bean

The soya bean is a useful food for vegetarians because it contains nearly as much protein as meat, and yet it has many different uses.

Soya beans can be cooked and eaten whole. The beans produce cooking oil, they make bean milk and bean curd, they are fermented to make soy sauce, and they are ground into high protein flour and used to make textured vegetable protein (see p. 11).

Questions
1 How and why should invalids be encouraged to eat nutritious foods?
2 Name the three types of vegetarian and list the foods each does *not* eat.
3 What protein foods could a vegan eat?

Homework
1 Find out about different ways of losing weight, by collecting articles and slimming diets. Describe one sensible way to lose weight.
2 Make up a day's menu for each of the following people: (a) an elderly housebound lady, (b) a pregnant woman, (c) a lacto-vegetarian (remember they do not eat meat or eggs), (d) a man on a slimming diet.
3 Find out about the slimmer's disease 'anorexia nervosa'.

Foods which have been prepared or processed to make cooking quicker and easier are known as **convenience foods**. We eat many convenience foods. Flour might be considered to be a convenience food because the wheat grain has been ground and sieved ready for use. However, we usually think of the following as convenience foods:

Canned food
Food is usually ready to eat from the can. Some foods need heating up to make a hot meal, e.g. baked beans, soup.

Frozen food
Whole meals can be frozen on a tray and cooked in the oven when required. Most foods can be frozen, e.g. fish fingers, pies, cakes, vegetables.

Dehydrated (dried) foods
Popular dried foods include soups, milk, and complete meals such as curry or paella in packets. Hot or cold water is added to make the food ready for use.

Vacuum packing
Boil-in-the-bag foods are vacuum packed and can be cooked entirely in the bag in boiling water.

Mixes
Food mixes can be quickly prepared by adding water or other ingredients. Examples are instant desserts, sauces, and cakes.

Why are convenience foods useful?

1 *They are easy to store*. Packets and tins are useful for unplanned meals.
2 *They save time*. Convenience foods can be prepared quickly and save time for the cook (e.g. frozen vegetables, ready-mix pastry).
3 *They save fuel and waste*. Cooking time is reduced, and very little food is wasted (e.g. boil-in-the-bag meals).
4 *They offer unusual dishes*. Convenience foods can be a quick way of preparing complicated and unusual dishes, e.g. Chinese food.

Are convenience foods bad for us?

Some convenience foods contain a lot of starch, sugar, and fat, and few other nutrients. These foods, which include snack foods like crisps and corn snacks, fill you up. You might eat them instead of a properly balanced meal.

If convenience foods are used for meals, it is important to include fresh fruit and vegetables too, to provide enough vitamin C and dietary fibre.

Convenience foods are often more expensive than fresh foods because they are prepared and packed before selling.

What's on the label?

When you buy fresh food you can see what you are getting. Convenience food is packed up and the description on the label is the only guide to what is inside.

Most packed food must display a complete list of ingredients, starting with the ingredient which weighs the most. Labels show the weight of the goods, and carry a name and address to write to for complaints. Any pictures must look like the food inside, and only that food — a picture of fish fingers and chips means that the packet contains fish fingers and chips! Some products show 'sell by' dates, to help you buy them in good condition.

Additives are listed on the label. These are chemicals which are added to food. They can improve the colour or texture, or help food to keep for longer. Additives include nutrients which improve food value. Scientists test the safety of additives in our food, and there are laws to say which ones can be used.

Ingredients when reconstituted:
Rice, beef, sultanas, onions, food starch, beef fat, apples, tomatoes, sugar, salt, curry powder, hydrolysed protein, citric acid, flavour enhancer (monosodium glutamate), colour (E 150), preservative (E 220) and antioxidant (E 320/E 321).

To do: Buy a complete dried meal. In a group, prepare the meal by following the instructions on the packet. Taste the meal and consider whether the packet meal was good value for money. List the ingredients on the packet. Did the picture on the packet look like the finished dish, and were there enough of each of the ingredients?

Questions
1 What are convenience foods, and what are the advantages and disadvantages of using them?
2 How could you prepare the following meals using only convenience foods?
   (a) shepherd's pie, mixed vegetables, sponge pudding and ice cream.
   (b) cod in parsley sauce, peas and chips, stewed plums and custard.
   (c) curry and rice, apple crumble and cream.
3 Make a list of some convenience foods which an elderly man could keep in his store cupboard to help him prepare meals for himself. Suggest a day's meals which he could prepare from this food if he were unable to go out shopping.

Homework
Visit your local supermarket. Make a list of the convenience foods available for: (a) completely prepared meals, (b) instant puddings, (c) snacks. Choose one product from each section, and make a list of its ingredients. Describe any other information on the packet.

Flavour and taste

Appetizing food should be attractive and have a pleasing flavour and smell. Flavour is a combination of taste and smell, sensed by the tongue and the nose.

Experiment to discover which parts of the tongue sense which flavours

Make up a solution of each of the following flavours:
1 salty water for salt taste
2 sugar and water for sweet taste
3 lemon juice for sour taste
4 instant coffee and water for bitter taste.

Use a straw to draw up some of the salty solution. Dip the solution from the straw on to the six areas of your tongue, as shown in the diagram. Write down which areas taste the salt. Repeat the test with a clean straw containing each of the other three solutions in turn. Draw the diagram of the tongue and label which parts sense the different tastes.

(The expected results are:
1 = bitter, 2 and 6 = sour, 3 and 5 = salt, 4 = sweet.)

Can people recognize food by its smell?

Ask a group of people to form a tasting panel. Collect some items with strong smells, e.g. chopped onion, almond and vanilla essence, pepper, ginger, cloves, dried rosemary, vinegar, and cheese. Label and cover each of the foods. Ask the panel to try and identify each of the items by its smell, without looking. When all of the panel have finished, mark the results.

Experiment to show that flavour is a combination of taste and smell

Hold your nose tightly with your fingers. Place a mint in your mouth and chew it. Let go of your nose and carry on chewing. Notice how the flavour increases once you are able to smell the food.

Crossword

Find the word in the green box.
The clue is: a carbohydrate.
Now fill in the answers to these clues:
1 Strict vegetarians (6)
2 Between the ages of 12 and 19, teenagers need extra food for their growth _____. (5)
3 To lose weight, _____ rich foods should be limited. (6)
4 The _____ of food is judged by taste and smell. (7)
5 Anorexia _____ is called the slimmers' disease. (7)

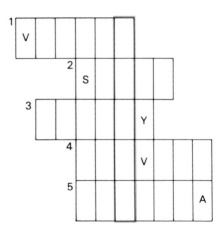

The shopping game

The shopping game needs a group of two or more people. The first player starts the game by saying 'I went shopping to buy some . . . .' and he names a group of foods, e.g. fruits, vegetables, cheeses, cuts of meat, dairy products, etc. The other players, in turn, call out their suggestions for foods in the named group. The game continues until there are no more suggestions, and the winner is the person with the last suggestion.

Questions
1 Choose one of the garnishes to add colour to each of the dishes listed below.
Garnishes: parsley, glacé cherry, tomato slices, chocolate buttons, lemon.
Dishes: cheese pie, tomato soup, instant dessert, grilled plaice, lemon meringue pie.
2 Use the *five* dishes above, and add other suitable dishes, to choose meals for the following:
(a) a picnic lunch for two boys who are going fishing.
(b) a three-course dinner for special guests.
(c) a hot meal for a hungry teenager.

Homework
1 Draw a plan of your local supermarket, to show the positions of the entrance and exit, the shelves, freezers, fridges, and cash registers. Label where different types of food are sold.

   The position of each food in a supermarket is usually carefully planned. Essential items, such as sugar, bread, tea, flour, eggs, and margarine, are often positioned so that the shopper has to travel around the shop to pick up these things, passing many tempting displays and special offers. At the cash desk there are often sweets and magazines. How has your supermarket planned the different positioning of its goods?

   'Eye level is buy level' is a slogan used by manufacturers and advertisers. Goods at eye level on the shelves are noticed first, and often sell best. Look at a supermarket display of biscuits. The tempting, more expensive, fancy biscuits are usually at eye level, and the plain biscuits lower down. Draw and label a picture of a biscuit display in your local supermarket.

2 Write a short piece about 'Food and shopping in the future', saying how you imagine shops and food will change over the next hundred years.

3. FOODS

EGGS (1)

In Britain we each eat, on average, four eggs a week. These come mostly from hens, although other birds, such as ducks and geese, also lay eggs which we can eat. The egg contains the food for the growing chick, so it is a very valuable food for us too.

What is an egg made of?

The egg provides food for body building and energy. It contains the minerals calcium and iron, which are needed for strong bones and healthy blood. The egg is a good source of vitamins A and D which help to keep us healthy.

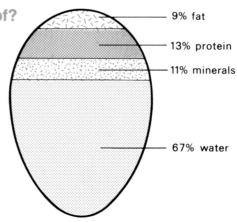

- 9% fat
- 13% protein
- 11% minerals
- 67% water

What does an egg look like inside?

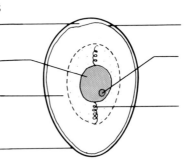

The **air sac** gets bigger as the egg gets older.

The **yolk** provides food for the young chick.

The **thick white** and **thin white** protect the chick.

The **shell** contains tiny holes so that the chick can breathe.

The **membrane** protects the inside of the egg.

The **germinal disc** is where the chick might begin to grow.

The **chalazae** are strings which keep the yolk in the middle of the egg.

Look for yourself

Crack an egg on a plate and see if you can find the thick and thin whites, the chalazae, and the germinal disc. Look into the empty shell and find the membrane and the air sac.

Cooking with eggs

Eggs have so many different uses in cooking that it would be very difficult to cook without them. Here are some of their uses.

1 Eggs can be used as a **main dish** in a meal, e.g. omelette.

2 Eggs **bind** dry ingredients so that they stick together when cooked, e.g. beefburgers.

3 Eggs **coat** foods, protecting them during frying, e.g. fish cakes.

4 When eggs are beaten, they **trap air**. The whole egg or just the white can be used, e.g. Swiss roll, meringue.

5 Eggs can **thicken** liquids, e.g. egg custard.

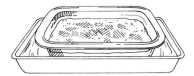

6 A beaten egg is used to **glaze** savoury pastry to make the surface shiny, e.g. sausage rolls.

7 An egg can be used to **enrich** dishes by adding extra nutrients, e.g. mashed potatoes.

8 Eggs can **garnish** dishes to make them attractive, e.g. sliced egg used in salad.

Eggs as beauty aids

Eggs are not only used in cooking!

To make a face mask for dry skins: mix an egg yolk with a little oil. Smooth on the face, leave for fifteen minutes, then rinse off with warm water.

For shining hair, wash the hair, then work in a beaten egg. Rinse very well, using cool water.

Questions

1 Cover the opposite page. Now draw an egg to show what it looks like inside.
2 Name two nutrients found in eggs, and say why each is important.
3 List the uses of eggs in cooking. Fit these examples into your list: (a) fried egg, (b) sponge flan, (c) soufflé, (d) Scotch eggs, (e) egg and bacon pie. Add some more dishes so that you have at least two examples under each heading.

Farming eggs

Hens start to lay their eggs when they are about five months old. They can produce about 300 eggs every year. The colour of the shell depends on the breed of hen. Usually brown hens produce brown eggs, and white hens produce white eggs. However, brown eggs are no better for us than white eggs.

Farmers can keep egg-laying hens in three different ways:

1 Free range farming

This means the hens are free to range all around the farm (and often further!) They pick up scattered food and sleep in a henhouse at night to protect them from foxes. Hens can get diseases from the soil, and in cold weather they will stop laying eggs.

2 Battery farming

Farmers need to choose the most efficient ways to produce food, because there are so many people to feed. Battery farming is the most popular method of egg farming and 97% of the eggs sold come from these farms. The hens are kept warm and well fed and will lay eggs all year round. Hens are kept in hen houses, which may contain as many as 1000 hens. Each cage could contain four to six hens. The hens never leave their cages. Food and water are provided, and the eggs roll down from the cages into collecting trays.

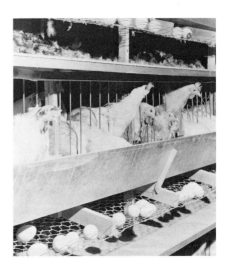

3 Deep-litter farming

Many hens live in a large shed and can move about on a floor covered with wood shavings or straw. The hens lay eggs in nest boxes, and food and water is provided for them.

With both battery and deep-litter farming, the farmer can make the winter day seem longer by leaving the lights on. This means that the hens lay more eggs because they think it is summer time.

Packing eggs

When eggs have been collected, they are taken to a packing station where they are examined for any faults. The eggs pass in front of a bright light, and any faults in the egg show up. A candle used to be used for this, and it is still called candling.

Candling eggs.

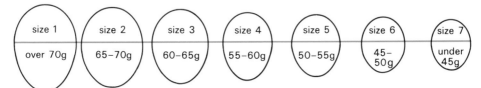

size 1	size 2	size 3	size 4	size 5	size 6	size 7
over 70g	65–70g	60–65g	55–60g	50–55g	45–50g	under 45g

The perfect eggs are then weighed, graded, and packed. The size of the egg depends upon its weight. The egg carton is designed to tell you where the egg comes from, when it was packed, and the size, the grade, number, and colour of the eggs inside.

How to store eggs

The tiny holes in the eggshell make it **porous**. This means that it will absorb liquids and smells. Eggs are best stored in a cool place, away from strong smelling foods like onions. The broad end of the egg should be at the top so that the yolk does not rest near the shell. This prevents the yolk from drying up.

As kitchens are very warm, eggs can be kept at the bottom of the fridge. When they are very cold it is difficult to whisk them, so they should be taken out in good time.

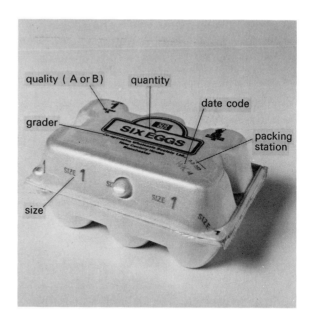

Questions

1 What are the different methods of farming eggs? Write down what is good and bad about each method.
2 Before packing, how is an egg examined?
3 How should an egg be stored? Why?
4 Why is the shell of an egg porous? What does porous mean?

39

How to test an egg for freshness

1 Place the egg in a glass of salty water. A fresh egg will sink, but a stale egg will float. This is because as an egg gets older, the air sac gets bigger, and the air makes the egg float.

  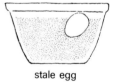

fresh egg   not so fresh   stale egg

2 Crack an egg on a plate. A fresh egg has three parts, a thin white, a thick white and a yolk. A stale egg looks flat.

fresh egg   not so fresh   stale egg

3 Smell the broken egg. A stale egg has a strong smell.

How to separate an egg into the white and the yolk

Make a firm crack in the middle of the egg with a knife.	Hold over a bowl and remove the top of the shell. Some of the white slips into the bowl.	Move the yolk carefully from one shell half to the other, leaving the white in the bowl.
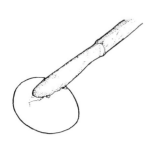	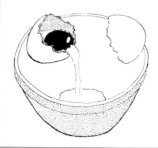	

Experiments with eggs

1 Separate an egg into the yolk and the white, as shown above.
(a) Place the white in a clean bowl and whisk it with a hand whisk or a fork. Notice how the white traps the air and gradually becomes dryer and stiffer.
(b) Try to whisk the yolk in the same way and notice what happens.
Use the egg to make scrambled egg.

2 Take one very fresh egg and one egg which is at least four weeks old. Test the eggs for freshness by placing them in a glass of salty water and seeing how they rest.
Now crack the eggs on a plate and look for the thin white, the thick white, and the yolk.

3 Boil two eggs for fifteen minutes. Place one
   to cool in cold water. Leave the other one to
   cool on its own. When cold, cut both eggs in
   half and notice the difference in colour. The
   hard-boiled egg which cooled on its own
   should have a dark ring around its yolk. This
   is because while the egg remains warm, the
   iron and sulphur in the egg combine to form
   a greyish-black ring of iron sulphide.

Fun with eggs

1 On a large floor space, roll an egg gently and notice how it returns to you as it
   might to the nest.
2 Hard boil an egg and find different ways of decorating the shell.

Easter Eggs

For Christians at Easter time, the egg was a
symbol of the Resurrection and was used at
Easter church services. In early times, the
church forbade the eating of eggs during
Lent. Because there were so many spare
eggs, the eggs were hard-boiled, painted, and
used for ball games. In the north of England
egg-rolling ceremonies still take place.
Chocolate eggs have now replaced the
coloured eggs.

Records

1 The heaviest hen's egg ever laid weighed 454 g (16 oz) and was laid in 1956. It
   had a double yolk and two shells.
2 The highest reported number of yolks in a chicken's egg is nine.
3 The greatest height from which an egg has ever been dropped, without
   breaking, was 198 metres from a helicopter, in October 1979.

Questions
1 Describe two ways to test an egg for freshness.
2 Which is best, a brown or a white egg?
3 Draw pictures to show how to crack an egg and separate it into the white and the
   yolk.

Homework
1 Find out the cost of different sizes of eggs in your local supermarket.
2 Draw and label a real egg carton and say what the information means.
3 Find out what the following are: (a) egg nog, (b) quiche lorraine, (c) omelettes,
   (d) Scotch eggs, (e) egg plant.
4 Make a list of the different birds' eggs we eat.

Milk is the first and most important food of many young animals. All female mammals produce milk to feed their young. In Britain, we drink a lot of cow's milk, but in other parts of the world, the milk from sheep, goats, camels, and even buffalo is used. A new-born baby often lives only on its mother's milk for several months, and look how it grows in that time!

The most popular breed of cow which is used for milk in Britain is the Friesian. These cows are black and white. A richer, creamier milk comes from the herds of Channel Island cows. These Guernsey and Jersey cows have soft brown coats, and lovely dark eyes.

Friesian cow.

Cows can eat up to 70 kg of grass a day, and the better the grass, the better the milk. The cows are milked twice a day, in the early morning and late afternoon. After calving, a cow can produce over twenty litres of milk a day.

Before the 1850s, clean milk was almost unknown. Town cows were kept in the back of milk shops and some were milked on the streets. The milk was often sour and dirty.

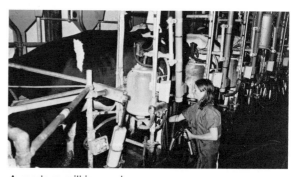

A modern milking parlour.

Nowadays, great care is taken to ensure that the milk is safe for us to drink. The herds of cows are treated to prevent them from carrying harmful bacteria. The farmer must take care that the milking parlour and all the equipment are kept very clean.

In many areas, milk is piped from the milking parlour into refrigerated stainless steel tanks. A road tanker collects this milk and takes it to the dairy.

Sterilized bottles are filled with milk at the bottling plant.

How was milk made safer?

About a hundred years ago, a French scientist called Louis Pasteur discovered that milk contained harmful bacteria. He found that by heating the milk to a certain temperature, the harmful bacteria were killed. He gave his name to this process: **pasteurization.**

Louis Pasteur.

How is milk treated today?

Milk can be treated in various ways to make it safe and to help it keep longer. Here are some of the ways in which this is done.

Pasteurized milk		Milk is heated to 71°C for fifteen seconds, then cooled rapidly. It will keep for four or five days in a fridge.
Homogenized milk		This is pasteurized milk which has the cream all mixed up in the milk, so that there is no cream line.
Sterilized milk		Homogenized milk is heated to 104°C for 20–30 minutes. This milk has a cooked taste and will keep, if not opened, for several weeks.
Ultra heat treated milk		Homogenized milk is heated to 132°C for one second, then cooled. It is called Long Life milk because it will keep, if not opened, for six months.
Dried milk		The water is driven out of the milk leaving a powder which will keep for six months. When water is added it tastes like fresh milk. It can be used in hot drinks.
Evaporated and condensed milk		Evaporated milk has 60% of its water removed and then it is canned. Condensed milk is evaporated milk with 50% sugar added to sweeten and preserve it.

Questions

1 Name six animals which produce milk.
2 How much grass does a cow eat in a day, and how many litres of milk might it produce?
3 What is pasteurization?
4 Fill in the missing words as you copy down this paragraph:
   P_____ milk is heated to 71°C for __ seconds then c_____. When milk has no cream line it is called h_____ milk. Milk which has been heated past boiling point and has a cooked taste is called s_____ milk. Long Life milk will keep for __ months if unopened. Its proper name is u_____ h_____ t_____ milk. Powdered milk is called _____ milk because it has its _____ removed.
5 What is the difference between condensed and evaporated milk?

43

Is milk the perfect food?

Milk is nearly a 'perfect food' because it contains some of all the nutrients needed for growth and health.

Milk is nearly 87% water. It contains protein for growth and repair. The fat and carbohydrate found in milk supply energy. Milk is a good source of calcium, but is a poor source of iron. It is rich in riboflavin (vitamin B), and contains vitamin A. Milk does not contain much vitamin C or D.

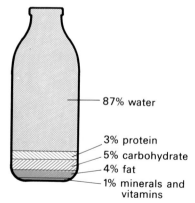

- 87% water
- 3% protein
- 5% carbohydrate
- 4% fat
- 1% minerals and vitamins

How does milk compare with other foods?

The **protein** in 1 pint of milk is equal to that in 3 eggs, or 100 g of meat.

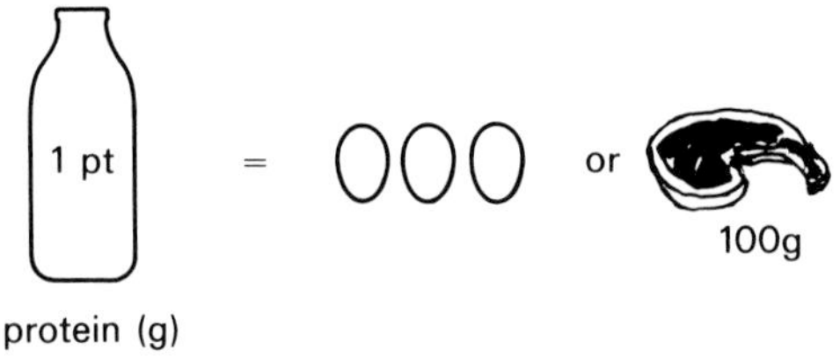

The **calcium** in 1 pint of milk is equal to that in 24 eggs, 17 kilos of potatoes, or 80 g of cheese.

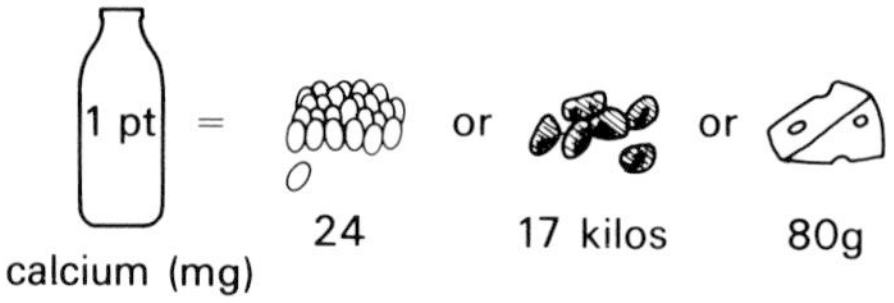

1 pt = 000 or 100g

protein (g)

1 pt = 24 or 17 kilos or 80g

calcium (mg)

Why is milk so useful?

Milk is delivered to 90% of homes in this country, and we each use, on average, two and half litres of milk a week. It is one of the cheapest and best quality foods there is.

It is a valuable and versatile food for all sorts of people:

Children need milk to help them grow big and strong.

Teenagers are growing rapidly, and need a lot of energy.

Pregnant women need milk for their baby to grow.

Old people may be too tired to cook, but can drink milk.

Milk makes delicious drinks, and can be used in many cooked dishes.

cakes   mashed potato   sauces   puddings   milk shakes

What can milk be made into?

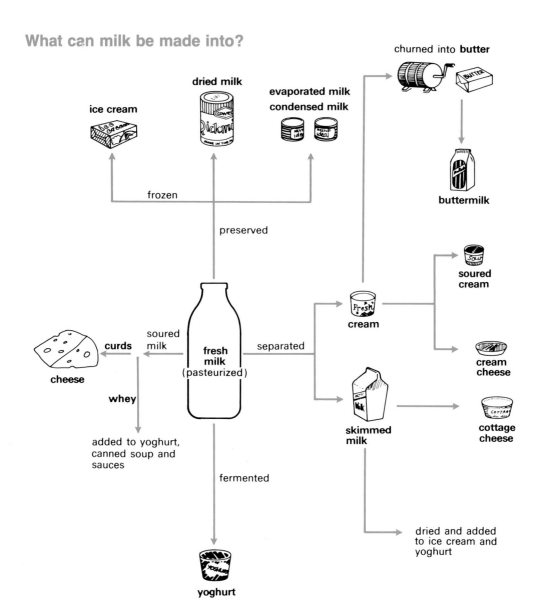

Questions

1 Copy out the following paragraph, and fill in the missing words:
   Milk is a good source of p_____ for growth and r_____. Milk is mostly made up of w_____ but contains some fat and c_____ for warmth and energy. It is a good source of the mineral c_____, needed for strong b_____. It also contains vitamins _____ and _____.
2 Why is milk a valuable food for (a) children, (b) old people, (c) teenagers?
3 Suggest some of your own ideas for milk dishes.
4 Use the chart above to find eight foods made from milk.

Cream

Cream can be skimmed from the top of the milk when it has been left to stand. Several types of cream can be bought. The thinnest cream is **single cream.** It is used for pouring over fruit or in coffee and contains 18% fat. **Whipping cream** and **double cream** are used to decorate dishes and contain 35–48% fat. The thickest cream is **clotted cream**, made in the South West of England. This contains at least 55% fat.

Butter

Butter is made from cream. The cream is placed in an enormous churn which can hold up to 1500 gallons of cream. The churn is turned to make the butter. The buttermilk separates out and runs away, leaving solid butter. Salt and colouring are sometimes added and then the butter is cut and packed. Salt gives the butter flavour and helps it to keep for longer.

Butter contains mostly fat and some vitamins A and D. It is delicious spread on bread, and is used in cooking for cakes and sauces.

A continuous buttermaker.

How to make your own butter

Put 300 ml double cream into a screw-top jar, with a clean marble, and shake until the cream is thick. Butter will suddenly be formed.

Strain off the buttermilk and use it as a drink. Wash the butter and add some salt to taste.

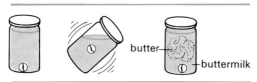

Yoghurt

Yoghurt is made from milk, and contains the goodness of milk. In a factory, yoghurt is made from homogenized milk, which is heated and cooled, and then special harmless bacteria are added. The mixture is kept warm for several hours, and becomes thick and slightly sour.

Yoghurt can be bought plain, or in fruit flavours. It is used in sweet and savoury dishes, and is a good food for children who do not like drinking milk.

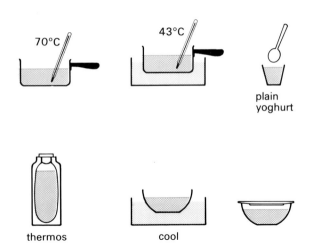

How to make your own yoghurt

Sterilize all the equipment by dipping it in boiling water. Heat one pint of milk in a pan and stir, until it reaches 70°C on a cooking thermometer. Take care not to break the thermometer!

Cool the milk to 43°C, by standing the pan in cold water. Add one tablespoon of fresh, plain yoghurt and pour into a thermos flask.

Leave for 6–8 hours until it thickens. Turn into a basin and cool. Cover with a plate and leave to thicken in the fridge for 4–6 hours.

Ice cream and its history

Ice cream was probably discovered in China. The Ancient Greeks made a delicious sweet from milk and honey which was chilled by mountain snow and stored in the ground to keep cold.

In the seventeenth century, Charles I's chef invented his own recipe for ice cream and the king rewarded him with £20 a year, as long as he kept the recipe a secret. When the king was beheaded, the chef fled to France and sold his recipe to the Café Napolitain, which gave its name to Neapolitan ice cream.

Guests of the American president, James Madison, were served frozen custard pies. A lady guest was so surprised, that she swore she had been poisoned, and had the chef arrested. The president's wife tried the pies and said they were delicious, and had the chef released.

Today, on average, each American eats twenty-four litres of ice cream a year!

Modern ice cream is made from fat, milk, and sugar, with flavourings and colour added. The most important ingredient is air. 50% of ice cream is made up of air! Ice cream is made by mixing all the ingredients, pasteurizing, homogenizing, and then freezing the mixture and whipping air into it.

Making caramel toffee ice cream.

Questions
1 What are the different types of cream for sale, and how are they used?
2 What is yoghurt?
3 What is ice cream made of?

Homework
1 Suggest ways in which an old lady could use milk to make a variety of meals.
2 Find out the meaning of these sayings: milk teeth, crying over spilt milk, milked for your money.

Cheese is made from milk with most of its water taken away. Cheese is usually made from cow's milk, but the milk from sheep and goats is sometimes used.

According to legend, Arab herdsmen discovered how to make cheese. The herdsmen carried the milk in bags made from sheep's stomachs, and they found that by the end of their journey the milk had turned into cheese! The heat from the sun must have turned the milk sour, and a substance called rennet, which is found in the sheep's stomach, helped to make this sour milk into cheese.

The Romans taught the Britons how to make cheese on a large scale. To begin with, cheese was given the name of the area where it was made. For example, Cheddar cheese was originally made in Cheddar gorge. Nowadays, the recipe for Cheddar cheese is copied by countries as far away as Canada and New Zealand.

How is cheese made?

1 Fresh milk is pasteurized, and a starter of special bacteria is added, to sour the milk. Later, rennet is added.

2 Solid curds and liquid whey are formed. The whey is drained off.

3 The curd is chopped and salted and then moulded and pressed to remove any excess whey. The cheese is then allowed to ripen. The flavour develops as the cheese gets older.

Adding rennet to milk.

Draining the whey.

How to make cheese yourself

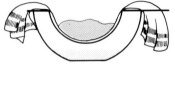

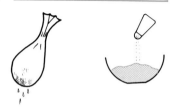

Take one pint of milk and either leave it to sour, or add two teaspoons of lemon juice and leave it overnight.

Strain the milk through a sieve lined with a tea-towel, so that the curds stay in the towel and the whey runs away.

Squeeze out any excess whey, then add some salt.

English cheeses

There are nine important English cheeses:

1 **Lancashire** A mild, white, crumbly cheese used in cooking.
2 **Cheshire** A crumbly cheese, orange or white in colour. This cheese was so popular with the Romans that they exported it to Italy.
3 **Wensleydale** A creamy cheese, which was once made by monks.
4 **Caerphilly** A mild, slightly salty cheese, popular in Wales.
5 **Cheddar** The best known cheese of all. It has a firm texture, and both mild and mature (strong) varieties can be bought.
6 **Stilton** A 'blue' cheese with a strong flavour. Sometimes called the 'King of cheeses'.
7 **Derby** A mild, smooth cheese.
8 **Double Gloucester** Quite a strong flavoured cheese, orange in colour.
9 **Leicester** A mild, crumbly cheese, deep orange in colour.

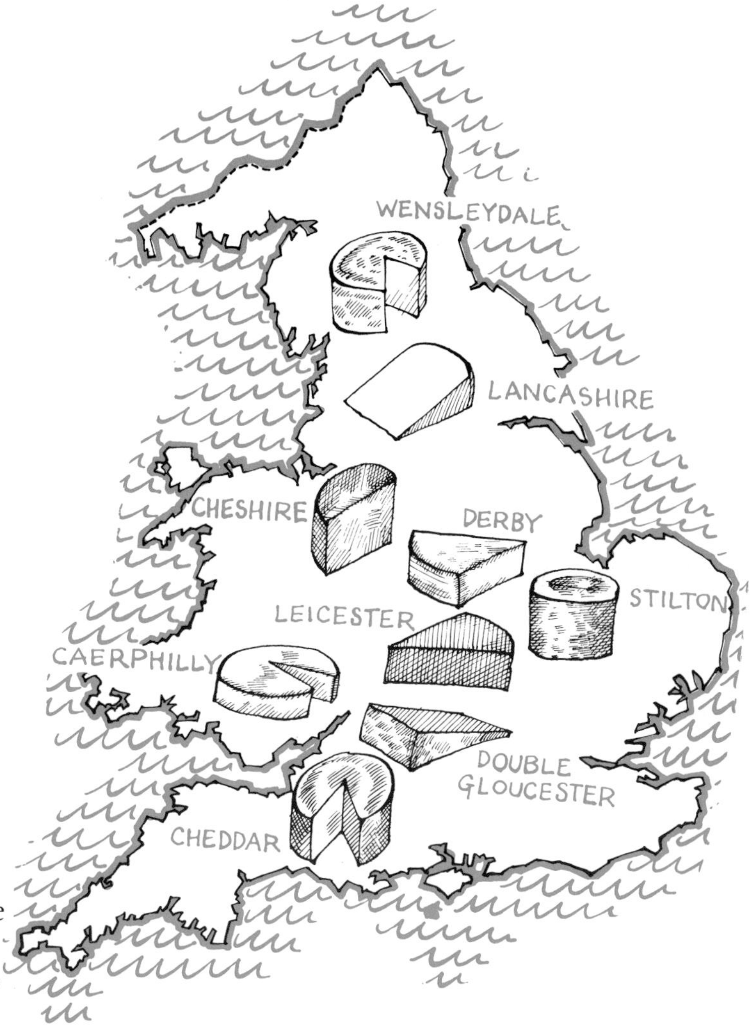

WENSLEYDALE

LANCASHIRE

CHESHIRE

DERBY

STILTON

LEICESTER

CAERPHILLY

DOUBLE GLOUCESTER

CHEDDAR

How to store cheese

Cheese is a living food, containing live bacteria, so it will change with age. Buy only as much as you need. Wrap it in foil and keep it in a polythene bag in the fridge. Take the cheese out of the fridge at least half an hour before you want to use it, so that the correct flavour can develop.

Questions

1 Copy out this paragraph and fill in the missing words:
Cheese is made from p_____ milk, and a s_____ is added to sour the milk. After rennet has been added, the milk forms c_____ and w_____. The curds are chopped and salted, and the w_____ runs away. The cheese is moulded and pressed and allowed to r_____.
2 Name nine famous English cheeses. Which is your favourite and why?

Questions about cheese

Q Why do some cheeses have holes in them?
A When the cheese is being made, a gas is produced, and the gas is trapped as bubbles.

Q Why is a cheese like Stilton called a 'blue' cheese?
A During the ripening of the cheese, blue mould begins to grow. This mould is harmless, and its growth is encouraged by inserting stainless steel needles.

Q What is the difference between cream cheese, curd cheese, and cottage cheese?
A **Cream cheese** is made from single or double cream.
Curd cheese is less rich, as it is made from milk.
Cottage cheese contains less fat, as it is made from skimmed milk, which has the fat rich cream removed.

Q Is it true that buffalo milk is used to make cheese?
A Yes. Buffalo milk makes a cheese called Mozzarella.

Q Why does some cheese have a rind on it?
A After the cheese is put into a mould, the moulds are sprayed with hot water. This produces the thin, hard rind which helps the cheese to keep longer.

Experiment: what happens when cheese is cooked?

1 Place 25 g of cheese on a metal plate under a hot grill. Watch closely as the cheese changes shape and melts. Cook the cheese a little longer, then cool it. When cool, notice how hard and dry the cheese is.

2 Chop up 25 g of cheese and boil it with 30 ml of milk in a saucepan. Notice how the cheese curdles the milk. This is the reason why cheese should only be added to a milk sauce *after* it is cooked.

What is the value of cheese?

One pint of milk (580 ml) produces only
60 g of cheese. Cheese is a nutritious food
because it is rich in protein, fat, calcium, and
vitamin A.

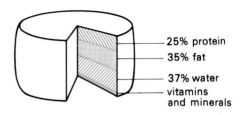

25% protein
35% fat
37% water
vitamins
and minerals

Cooking with cheese

Cheese is very useful because it is easy to
prepare and there is very little waste. Cheese
can be eaten raw in sandwiches and salads.
It can also be cooked and made into simple,
delicious dishes, such as macaroni cheese.
Cottage or cream cheese can be used to
make sweet cheesecakes.

Records

1 More cheese is eaten in France than in any
  other country. In 1979 each Frenchman ate,
  on average, 17.3 kilograms of cheese. In the
  United Kingdom, in that year, we each ate
  5.66 kilograms of cheese.

2 The most expensive cheese in the world is
  La Baratte, made in France. It costs £20.70
  per kilo.

Set up a cheese-tasting panel

Buy small portions (100 g) of as many
different cheeses as you can afford. Make a
chart with the following headings: (a)
cheese, (b) appearance, (c) taste, and (d)
marks out of ten. Taste each of your cheeses
and fill in the chart.

Try some cheeses from other countries.
Some have coloured rinds, e.g. Edam.
Some have holes in them, e.g. Gruyère.
Some are soft to eat, e.g. Brie.

Edam cheese can have a red or
yellow rind.

Questions

1 What are the nutrients found in cheese?
2 At which meal times would you serve the following cheese dishes: (a) cheese and
  bacon pie, (b) cheese on toast, (c) cheesecake? What other foods would you serve to
  complete each meal?
3 When would you add cheese to a milk sauce, and why?

Homework

Start a project on 'Famous cheeses'. Find out about different cheeses from all over
the world. Visit your local supermarket and find out what selection of cheeses they
have for sale. Buy and taste some foreign cheeses, and find some recipes in which
you can use them.

Primitive people hunted wild animals for meat. As people learned to farm the land, they kept and reared animals to provide milk and meat.

Domesticated animals, such as pigs, sheep, and cows, are valuable to the farmer. Over the years, farmers have chosen their best animals for breeding to improve the quality of their herds. Most people prefer leaner, tender meat, so by careful breeding and feeding, farmers can produce the kind of meat which the public wants to buy.

Animals used for meat

Beef and veal

Most beef comes from young bullocks. Female calves are fatter, and the farmer may keep them for milking and to produce more calves. The older animals have a tougher, drier flesh, and this needs careful cooking. Veal comes from calves three to four months old.

Beef cattle.

Lamb and mutton

Sheep are raised for both wool and meat. There are many different breeds of sheep. Some live off rich pastureland and others eat poor mountain grass. Lamb comes from an animal which is less than one year old. Mutton comes from older animals.

A flock of Hampshire Down sheep.

Pork and bacon

A pig grows quickly and can produce many piglets. A female pig can have sixteen piglets a year, and a pig may be slaughtered when it is sixteen weeks old. At this age it could weigh 59 kilos. Pigs are often kept in large, warm, clean sheds, and fed on special food.

A bacon pig is larger and leaner than the pork pig. The meat is salted in brine, and then smoked. Green bacon is salted but not smoked.

Pigs can produce many piglets.

The value of meat

Meat is a good source of protein, iron, and the B vitamins. Meat varies in the amount of fat it contains.

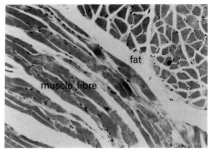

What is meat made up of?

Lean meat is made of bundles of muscle fibres, all bound together by **connective tissue**. Tougher meat comes from older animals and well worked muscles.

The structure of meat.

To do: Take a small piece of meat, such as shin or skirt of beef, and examine the structure of the muscle using a hand lens.

Why do we cook meat?

1 Meat is cooked to kill bacteria and make the meat safe to eat.
2 Cooking makes meat tender and easier to eat.
3 Cooking improves the flavour of meat.

How to choose meat

Supermarkets and butchers' shops sell meat. A butcher can help you decide what to buy, and advise you on how to cook it. In supermarkets, the meat is wrapped, and the label tells you the weight, the price, and the cut of meat. Choose meat with a fresh smell, firm and moist flesh, and not too much fat.

How to store meat

Fresh meat should be unwrapped, then put on a plate and covered with foil or cling wrap. It will keep in the coldest part of the fridge for up to three days. Mince should be eaten or cooked on the day of purchase. Meat can be frozen and kept in the freezer. Care must be taken to wrap and label it properly.

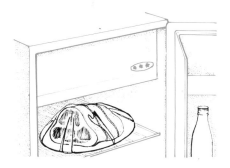

Food tales

King Charles I had lost his way after a day's hunting in Epping forest. He came across a group roasting an ox, and was so pleased to have shared their feast, that he knighted the meat 'Sir Loin'.

Questions

1 Name *three* animals which are reared for their meat, and the meat we get from them. Name *two* dishes which can be made with each type of meat.
2 Write, in your own words, some advice about buying and storing meat.
3 Why is meat cooked?

53

Offal

Offal is the name given to the internal organs and pieces which are trimmed off from the dead animal. All kinds of foods such as pâtés, haggis, faggots, and sausages are made from offal.

Why is offal good for us?

Liver, kidney, and heart all contain as much protein as meat. They are rich in iron and the B vitamins. Liver is a good source of vitamin A.

Types of offal

Liver Lambs' liver can be fried or grilled. Ox and pigs' livers are used to make pâté.	**Kidneys** should be well washed before cooking. Small kidneys can be grilled or fried.	**Hearts** need gentle cooking, and can be filled with a savoury stuffing.
Brains Long ago, brains were eaten because they were thought to make you clever!	**Tripe** is the stomach of the ox, which has been cleaned and prepared before selling.	**Head** In the Middle Ages, the pig's head was the main dish at a feast. Pies and brawn are made from this meat.

The **tail** is cooked to make oxtail soup. **Feet** are eaten, particularly pigs' trotters, and the **tongue** is cooked, pressed, and sliced.

Sausages

Recipes for sausages have been known for hundreds of years. In a monk's recipe book of 1450, his sausage was made from ground pork mixed with egg and seasoning. This mixture was stuffed into the neck of a chicken and roasted.

In 1786, John Wall opened a pork butcher's shop in London. The sausages were so good that he was appointed to supply them for King George III. His sausage recipe is still popular today.

Today, by law, an English pork sausage must contain 65% meat. Sausage meat is made from meat, cereal, water and seasoning, which is stuffed into the animal intestine or special sausage skins, then twisted into sausages.

Pork sausages being packed.

Poultry

Poultry, such as chicken and turkey, used to be eaten only on special occasions, such as Christmas. With modern farming methods, chicken has become cheap enough to eat all the time. Thousands of birds can be reared in battery cages or deep-litter sheds, just like the egg-laying birds.

Poultry is a valuable food because it contains as much protein as meat, as well as B vitamins and a little iron. Chicken and turkey contain less fat than other meat.

A Christmas turkey.

Warning

Poultry can contain the food-poisoning bacteria, salmonella. Live salmonella bacteria can make you ill. If the chicken is properly cooked, the bacteria will be killed and cannot harm you. Frozen chickens should always be defrosted before they are cooked. If they are cooked from frozen, the inside could be raw when the outside is well done. The raw meat could contain live bacteria.

Inside a chicken-processing factory.

To store poultry

Place the bird on a plate, and cover with cling wrap or foil. The bird can be kept at the top of the fridge for up to three days.

Game

Wild birds caught for food, such as pheasant or partridge, are called 'game'. So are animals such as deer and hare. Game is often hung up for several days so that the meat becomes more tender and the flavour improves.

Records

The record time for plucking chickens: four women plucked 12 chickens in 32.9 seconds.

Pheasants left to hang.

Questions
1 Decode the names of these types of offal: reliv, narib, dahe, dekniys, rthae, repti.
2 Name three nutrients found in offal and say why each is important.
3 Why must poultry be properly defrosted before cooking?

Homework
Draw the outlines of the three animals: beef, pig, and lamb. Find out how each animal is divided into cuts of meat. For each animal find out the cost of two cuts of meat, and suggest how to cook them.

55

FISH

Most fish live in the sea. Fish which live near the bottom of the sea, such as plaice and cod, are caught by the nets from trawlers. These nets are dragged above the sea bed to catch the fish. Fish which live near the surface, like herring and mackerel, are caught by drift nets. Crabs and lobsters can be caught in wicker pots left on the sea bed. Other shellfish can be scooped up from the sea bed.

White fish and oily fish

White fish get their name from their white flesh. It is white because it contains very little fat. White fish store most of their fat in their livers. We extract this fat to make products like cod-liver oil. Oily fish contain fat in their flesh. The flesh is often darker than that of white fish.

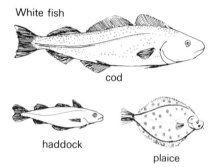

White fish

cod

haddock

plaice

Why is fish good for us?

Fish contains nearly as much protein as meat, and so is a good body-building food. White fish contains very little fat, but oily fish is rich in fat and so is a good energy food. Oily fish contains vitamins A and D in its fat. Some fish, such as sardines, can be canned. This makes their bones soft enough to eat, and these bones supply us with calcium.

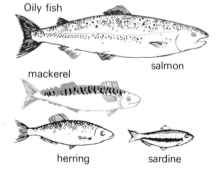

Oily fish

salmon

mackerel

herring

sardine

Shellfish

There are two main types of shellfish, crustacea and molluscs.
Crustacea, such as crabs, lobsters, prawns, and shrimps, have legs and an outside shell. We eat the inside of the tail and claws.
Molluscs, such as cockles, winkles, and mussels, have just a shell and no legs.
Fresh shellfish should be chosen carefully. Do not buy them if they smell strange. Eat them soon after you have bought them, as they do not keep long. Prawns and other shellfish can also be bought frozen or in cans.

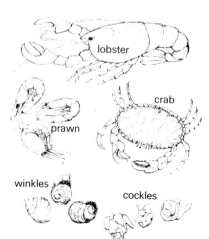

lobster

crab

prawn

winkles

cockles

Smoked fish

Smoking fish is a method of preserving them. The fish are hung in the smoke of special wood fires for several hours. Well-known smoked fish are kippers (smoked herrings), smoked salmon, and smoked mackerel.

Shopping for fish

Fresh fish needs to be chosen carefully, as it does not keep long. There are five important points to remember when buying fish:

1 Make sure that the shop is clean.
2 Choose fish with a fresh smell.
3 The fish should be firm, not limp.
4 The eyes should be shiny and bright.
5 The gills should be bright red.

Preparing fish for smoking.

Frozen fish is easy and convenient to buy. Sometimes it has been made into fish fingers or coated in breadcrumbs or batter.

Eat fresh fish as soon as possible after buying it. Store it at the top of the fridge.

How can fish be cooked?

Fish can be cooked easily and quickly. White fish does not have a strong flavour and it can be cooked with a cheese sauce or tomatoes. The most popular way to cook white fish is to fry it. Oily fish can be grilled, fried, or baked.

A fish display in a supermarket.

Fact and fiction

The roe or eggs of the sturgeon are called caviar, and in 1983 the best caviar cost £320 a kilo.

Why is the plaice dark and spotted on one side, and white on the other? The story goes that Moses was cooking some plaice over an open fire, and the fire went out. He was so cross that he threw the fish back into the sea, half cooked. The fish came to life and to this day it swims with one burned side.

Questions
1 Write the following headings: **white fish, oily fish, shellfish**. Put these fish under the correct heading: lobster, cod, plaice, herring, sardine, haddock, cockle, mackerel.
2 What is the difference between white fish and oily fish?
3 Name three nutrients found in fish and say why each is important.

Homework
Find out the cost per pound of each of the following fish: cod, herring, smoked mackerel. Describe the fish, and suggest two different meals you could make with each of them.

FRUIT AND VEGETABLES (1)

What is the difference between fruit and vegetables?

Science books will tell you that a fruit contains the seeds of the new plant. Tomatoes and cucumbers are really fruits. In the kitchen, we sometimes group things differently, and we expect fruit to be served as a sweet food, and vegetables with salt and pepper. Rhubarb is cooked with sugar, and so thought to be a fruit, but strictly it is a vegetable!

Vegetables

The groups of vegetables are named after the different parts of the plant.

Vegetable fruits
marrows
cucumbers
pumpkins

Stems and leaves
celery
spinach
lettuce

Seeds and flowers
peas
beans
cauliflower

Roots, tubers and bulbs
swedes
potatoes
onions

Try and add some of the following examples to the groups: leeks, turnips, broccoli, tomatoes, spring greens, carrots, radishes.

What makes up a plant?

A plant needs to feed and grow, and produce seeds for more plants. The roots absorb valuable nitrogen and minerals from the soil. The leaves of the plant are able to change carbon dioxide and water into carbohydrates. This process is called **photosynthesis**. The green plant uses the energy from the sun. The plant walls contain cellulose, which gives the plant its shape. A lot of the plant is made of water, and this keeps the plant rigid.

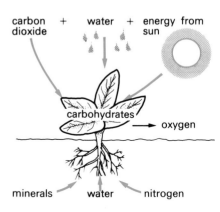

The value of vegetables

Different groups of vegetables can give us different nutrients:

Green leafy vegetables provide vitamin C, and vitamin A in the form of carotene, as well as dietary fibre.

Root vegetables contain a little vitamin C, some vitamin A, and carbohydrates.

Seed vegetables are a source of protein, carbohydrate, vitamin C, and dietary fibre.

How to choose vegetables

Fresh vegetables should be clean and free from soil. The leaves should be bright in colour, and should not look wilted or damaged. It is cheaper to buy the vegetables when they are in season, and they will have a better flavour too.

How to store vegetables

Fresh green vegetables can be kept somewhere cool, e.g. in the bottom of the fridge, for a short time.

Root vegetables should be stored in a cool, dark place. Potatoes should not be used if they are turning green.

Frozen vegetables should be kept in the freezer or icebox. Because they are frozen soon after picking, they contain as many nutrients as fresh vegetables.

Canned and dried vegetables should be stored in a dry place. Rusty or dented tins should not be used.

Experiment to find out how long to cook vegetables

Tear up the leaves of 100 g of green cabbage and divide them into three equal portions. Boil 150 ml water in each of three saucepans with a pinch of salt. Add the cabbage to each of the pans. Cook one for two minutes, then drain; cook the second for five minutes, and the third for ten minutes. Taste the results and decide which you like the best.

2 minutes   5 minutes   10 minutes

Questions

1 Copy out the following paragraph and fill in the missing words:
   Plants grow because roots absorb goodness from the s____, and leaves can make carbohydrates by the process of p_____. Plant walls are made up of c_____ and the plant is kept rigid by w_____. Vegetables provide large amounts of vitamin __ as well as vitamin A in the form of c_____. They are useful sources of dietary f_____.
2 Decode the name of each vegetable and decide which part of a plant it is:
   relcey, epa, racrot, eban, wesde, celttue, rromaw.
3 How would you store the following in the kitchen:
   carrots, frozen beans, cabbage, tinned peas?
4 What nutrients are found in the following groups of vegetables:
   green leafy vegetables, root vegetables, seed vegetables?
5 Give two examples for each of the following groups of vegetables: (a) green leafy vegetables, (b) root vegetables, (c) seed vegetables.

Vitamin C: See it – Save it!

Vitamin C is essential for good health, and fresh fruit and vegetables are the most important source of this vitamin. Vitamin C is easily destroyed, so great care should be taken when preparing fruit and vegetables.

This is the best way to cook fruit and vegetables:

Boil a little water in a saucepan. Add salt for vegetables.

Prepare the fresh vegetables or fruit *quickly*.

Plunge them into the boiling water and cook until ready.

Serve and eat immediately. Use the cooking water for gravy or sauce.

Vitamin C must be saved! Follow these rules and **Save it**

Do *not* buy old and wilted vegetables.

Do *not* soak vegetables and fruit. The vitamin C will dissolve in the water.

Do *not* chop vegetables too finely before cooking. It is better to tear up leafy vegetables.

Do *not* start to cook vegetables in lots of *cold* water. They will take longer to cook and lose more vitamin C.

Never add bicarbonate of soda to cooking water as this will destroy some vitamin C.

Do *not* leave vegetables to stand too long before serving.

Each of these weights of vegetables will provide our daily requirement of 30 mg of vitamin C:

75g boiled Brussels sprouts   150g cooked green cabbage   55g raw green cabbage   200g boiled peas   50g watercress

Billions of beans

The first tin of baked beans was produced in America in 1895. The tins contained a piece of pork for flavour, and were a luxury food in England because they were so expensive. Baked beans were first manufactured in England in 1928, and as the cost began to fall they became popular. Now, nearly one billion tins of beans are sold each year.

Are baked beans good for us?
A 225 g tin of beans can provide over one sixth of the protein needed daily, as well as some calcium and iron. The protein value of beans is increased if they are eaten with bread.

Potatoes

Sir Walter Raleigh brought potatoes to Britain in the 16th century, but it took 200 years before people became interested in growing them. Now they are our most popular vegetable, and we each eat nearly one kilo a week. Because we eat so many, potatoes supply us with nearly a quarter of our daily needs for vitamin C.

The Second World War made it very difficult to import food from overseas, so the Government started a 'Dig for Victory' campaign. Back gardens and city squares were planted with vegetables, especially potatoes, and everyone was told to eat a pound of potatoes a day.

Potatoes are sometimes thought to be fattening foods. It is the fat the potatoes are cooked in which increases the Calories. Look at the difference in Calories between boiled potatoes, chips and roast potatoes.

WOMEN! Farmers can't grow all your vegetables

BROCCOLI
POTATOES
CABBAGE
WHEAT
ONIONS
FODDER FOR DAIRY COWS
BRUSSELS SPROUTS
BARLEY for BREAD

You must grow your own. Farmers are growing more of the other essential crops — potatoes, corn for your bread, and food for the cows. It's up to you to provide the vegetables that are vital to your children's health — especially in winter. Grow all you can. If you don't, they may go short. Turn your garden over to vegetables. Get the older children to help you. If you haven't a garden ask your local council for an allotment. DO IT NOW.

DIG for Victory
ISSUED BY THE MINISTRY OF AGRICULTURE

Calories for every 100g potatoes

roast potatoes 111 kcal

chips 236 kcal

boiled potatoes 80 kcal

Records

The largest tomato ever grown weighed 2.94 kg and the largest carrot weighed 3.5 kg.

To do: Grow some seeds to eat with salad. Put some mung beans or mustard and cress seeds in a jam jar with some damp paper, and keep them moist until they sprout. Wash and eat the sprouts. Seeds contain protein and are able to grow into new plants.

Questions
1 Explain how you would cook a cabbage to avoid losing too much vitamin C.
2 List *eight* different ways of serving potatoes, e.g. crisps.
3 Use each of these groups of vegetables in different meals: (a) chips and tomatoes, (b) swedes and cabbage, (c) lettuce and cucumber, (d) onions, peas, and beans.

Fruit

Fruit contains the seeds of the plant. Sometimes you can eat the seeds – peanuts and pomegranates, for example – but often the seeds are too hard to eat, like the pips of oranges and apples.

There are different groups of fruit:

Citrus fruit comes from hot countries, particularly those around the Mediterranean sea. Citrus fruit includes oranges, grapefruit, lemons, and satsumas. They are an excellent source of vitamin C, and so these fruits were carried on board sailing ships to prevent the sailors from getting scurvy on long sea voyages (see p. 15). Citrus fruits should be bought when they are firm and bright, and should be eaten before the skins start to wither.

Soft fruit includes raspberries, strawberries, gooseberries, and blackcurrants. Because they are soft to touch, these fruits should be handled gently, and eaten soon after they have been picked. Be careful not to buy any mouldy fruits as they will affect others which they touch.

Tree fruit includes apples, pears, and fruit containing stones, such as peaches and plums. Many of these fruits are grown in Britain, and they are better value when they are bought in season. Apples and pears will store well if kept cool. Stone fruit should be eaten soon after purchase.

Exotic fruit. Nowadays, fruit can be transported by air or sea, and stays fresh and in good condition. Fruits from other countries can add variety, and can be used when home-grown fruit is not in season. Popular exotic fruits include bananas, pineapples, melons, and grapes.

Dried fruit. Dried grapes have been used for many years during the winter months when fresh fruit is scarce. Dried fruit is very sweet, and can be used instead of sugar. Dried grapes are called sultanas, raisins, and currants. Figs and dates can be dried too.

The value of fruit

Fruit is an important source of **vitamin C**, and contains some **dietary fibre**. A teenager or adult needs 30 mg of vitamin C daily. Here are some fruits which can supply this amount:

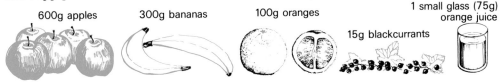

600g apples 300g bananas 100g oranges 15g blackcurrants 1 small glass (75g) orange juice

Crisp fruits such as apples and hard pears help to clean the teeth. It is better to eat fresh fruit rather than chocolates and sweets. Fruit can be eaten instead of puddings by people who need to lose weight.

Ways to keep fruit

Fresh fruit should be kept in a cool room. Fruit is often **canned** in a heavy sugar syrup which makes it much sweeter than the fresh fruit. Fruit loses some of its vitamin C when it is canned.

Frozen fruit may contain nearly as much vitamin C as the fresh fruit.

Fruit can be **dried**, and can be made into jams, jellies, and marmalade.

To do: Prepare a fresh fruit salad from a banana, an apple, an orange, and some lemon juice. Look at the structure of each fruit as you cut it up. A hand lens will help you see in more detail. Toss half the fruit in the lemon juice, and leave half uncovered. After ten minutes compare the two mixtures. What has happened?

Why does the uncovered fruit turn brown?
The air reacts with the cut fruit and changes its colour. The lemon juice protects the other fruit from turning brown.

Which is the best buy?

Visit your local shops and buy half a kilo each of the most *expensive* and the *cheapest* apples and green vegetables in season. Compare quality, appearance, and taste of your purchases and say which you think is the best buy.

Questions
1 Copy out the following paragraph and fill in the missing words:
   Fruits are valuable sources of vitamin __. They also contain dietary f_____. _____ fruit can help to clean our teeth.
2 Why is an orange a day better for you than an apple?
3 Decode the name of each fruit and decide if it is a citrus fruit or a stone fruit:
   garone, mile, eacph, rrhcey, mulp, moeln.

Homework
Start a project on 'Fruit and vegetables'. Choose *ten* fruits and *ten* vegetables. Find out where the fruits and vegetables are grown and when they are in season. Draw a picture of each fruit and vegetable and describe how to prepare it for eating.

CEREALS (1)

Ancient people picked the seeds of wild grasses for food. Eventually they discovered that it was easier to sow and harvest their own seeds, and then they could grow the grass they liked the best.

Cereals are the seeds of grasses, grown for eating. They get their name from Ceres, the goddess of the harvest. Nowadays, farmers and scientists work together to try to produce the best possible harvest.

Here are six important cereals:

Wheat

Nomadic tribes brought wheat seeds from the Middle East to Europe. Wheat was brought to Britain in about 2000 BC. Wheat can be grown all over the world.

Uses: Wheat is normally milled into flour and used for cakes, bread, and pastries. It can be made into breakfast cereal and pasta.

Rye

When wheat was introduced into Europe, it arrived with lots of weeds, and among these was rye. Rye liked the cold climate and poor soil of Northern Europe and grew faster and taller than the wheat.

Uses: Rye is used to make a thin, dry crispbread and black rye bread.

Rice

Rice has been grown for thousands of years in Eastern countries such as China, India, and Pakistan. The story is told that when a spice ship, bound for England, took refuge at a port in North America, the captain left a bag of rice seed as thanks. Rice has been grown in America ever since.

Uses: The two main kinds of rice used in Britain are long grain rice, used with curries and savoury dishes, and short, round grain rice used for puddings.

Maize

Maize is better known as sweetcorn. It has been grown in South America since 2000 BC. Sir Walter Raleigh brought it to England to show to his queen, Elizabeth I. The settlers in North America were saved from famine because the Indians showed them how to plant maize. America now grows most of the world's maize.

Uses: Maize is used for cornflour, custard powder, breakfast cereals, and popcorn. Sweetcorn is eaten as a vegetable, and the corn is crushed for oil.

Oats

Oats grow in cooler, wetter climates and are popular in Scotland and the North of England. Seeds used to be used instead of money, and the oat seed gave its name to a coin, 'the groat'. Oats were taken by settlers to North America.

Uses: Oats can be used to make porridge and breakfast cereals. They are also used for animal food.

Barley

The seed planted for harvesting was often a mixture of different cereals. The barley seeds grew well on poor soil where the wheat would die. Barley is grown in all parts of Britain.

Uses: Barley can be eaten in the form of pearl barley, for example, in soups; but more often it is used to make beer and whisky. A lot is used for animal feed.

When a cereal grows well in an area, it becomes the **staple food** of the people living there. A staple food is one which forms the largest part of the diet.

Wheat is the staple food in Britain, because we eat a lot of bread, cakes, and biscuits. Rice is the staple food for about half the world's population, in areas such as China and India.

Cereals are important in our diet because they supply one third of our energy needs. They contain valuable amounts of carbohydrate, a little protein, calcium, and iron, and some of the B vitamins.

What wheat looks like

If you cut open a wheat grain and look at it under the microscope, you will be able to see the different parts.

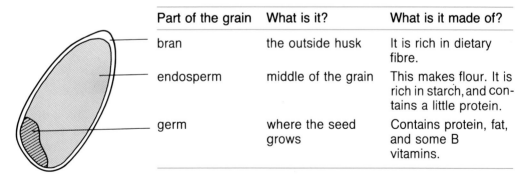

Part of the grain	What is it?	What is it made of?
bran	the outside husk	It is rich in dietary fibre.
endosperm	middle of the grain	This makes flour. It is rich in starch, and contains a little protein.
germ	where the seed grows	Contains protein, fat, and some B vitamins.

Questions

1 Decode the name of these cereals, and suggest a dish you could make with each one: toas, yarlbe, hetwa, cire, zamie, yre.

2 Fill in the missing words when you copy out these sentences:
The b_____ is the outside husk of the wheat grain, and is rich in d_____ f_____. The endosperm is the m_____ of the grain and is rich in s_____. It makes f_____. The seed grows from the g_____ which contains p_____ and f_____ and v_____.

3 From which cereals are each of these foods made: cornflakes, porridge, bread, beer?

How is flour made?

Flour used to be made by grinding the wheat grains with a hand mill.

Try crushing a few grains of wheat yourself, using a rolling pin.

Nowadays, most of our flour is made at the flour mills.

1 The wheat is dry cleaned to remove unwanted dust and soil.

2 The clean grains are then 'milled', which means the grain is opened up by rollers.

3 The bran comes off in large flakes and is sieved out and collected. A coarse flour called semolina is left.

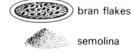

bran flakes

semolina

4 This flour passes through rollers and is sieved to make a smooth, fine flour.

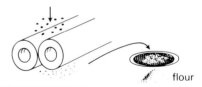

flour

What sort of flour shall I use?

Here are some of the flours that can be bought in the shops.

Plain white flour
To make white flour, 30% of the wheat grain is removed. Both the bran and the germ are taken out.

Plain white flour is used for cakes, sauces, and pastry.

Self-raising flour
Chemicals are added to this flour so that the mixture will rise when it is cooking. This saves the cook the bother of measuring out the baking powder or bicarbonate of soda. This flour is used for cakes, scones, and biscuits.

Wholemeal flour
This flour is made by crushing the whole of the grain. Nothing is added or taken away. It is brown in colour and quite gritty to feel.

This flour can be used for pastry, bread, scones, and cakes. Foods made with wholemeal flour contain more dietary fibre than those made with white flour.

Strong flour
Strong flour is made from a special strong wheat, which is grown in North America. It is used to make bread and pastries such as flaky pastry.

Investigating flour

Take some plain white, strong, and self-raising flour.

1 Mix 100 g of each flour with enough water to form a stiff ball of dough. This dough should be dry and not sticky. Knead it together like pastry.

2 This ball of dough can be either: (a) wrapped and tied in a piece of muslin, or (b) held carefully in the hands.

3 Hold the dough under the tap and run water over the dough. Notice how the white **starch** dissolves out into the water.

4 Squeeze and work the dough until no more starch will come out. This could take ten minutes.

5 The dough should look like a piece of old chewing gum with no pockets of starch. This dough contains a substance called **gluten**.

6 Bake each gluten ball in a hot oven, 220°C, 425°F, Gas 7. Each ball should puff up in the oven. The more protein there is in the flour, the bigger the gluten ball which can be made.

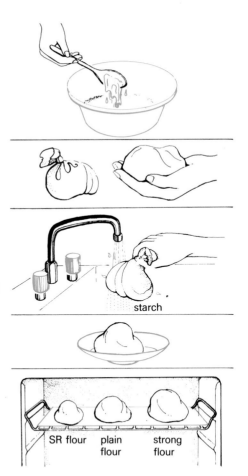

starch

SR flour   plain   strong
             flour   flour

The food value of bread

In Britain, we each eat, on average, nearly three small loaves a week. This means that bread is an important part of our diet. Bread is a valuable source of nutrients, and contains carbohydrate for energy, some protein, iron, calcium, and some of the B vitamins.

We eat a lot more white bread than brown bread. In the past, white bread was eaten by the rich people, and so people thought of white bread as a luxury.

Wholemeal bread is rich in dietary fibre, because the whole of the grain is used. This dietary fibre is important in preventing constipation. White bread contains less dietary fibre than wholemeal bread, but it has special nutrients, such as calcium, added to make up for losses during milling. Both white and wholemeal bread are useful, cheap foods.

Questions
1 How does a grain of wheat become flour? Draw some pictures to illustrate your answer.
2 What is the difference between wholemeal flour and white flour?
3 Give the names of four different flours and suggest a dish that can be made with each one.
4 Why is bread important in our diet? What can be made from bread?

Pasta

Pasta is made from a special wheat called durum wheat. The Chinese people were eating pasta nearly 6000 years ago. From his travels to the East, the explorer Marco Polo is thought to have brought pasta to Italy. The Italians made pasta famous with delicious dishes like spaghetti bolognese and lasagne.

To make pasta the wheat is ground and mixed with water to form a paste.

This paste can be made into lots of different shapes.

Pasta is cooked in boiling salted water for between five and fifteen minutes, depending on its size.

Whole grain cereals and refined cereals

Many cereal products can now be bought which use the whole of the grain. These are thought to be good for us to eat because they are rich in dietary fibre.

A **refined** cereal has the outer parts of the grain removed.

Whole grain products.   Refined cereal products.

Storing cereals

All cereals should be stored in a cool, dry place. If the packet is not very strong, store cereals in jars, or plastic containers with tight-fitting lids.

Plain flour will keep for four to six months, but wholemeal flours will only keep for two months and then they turn sour.

The discovery of breakfast cereals

It was in the early 1900s, in America, that two brothers discovered that maize could be steamed and rolled into flakes. The brothers were called Kellogg and they called their invention cornflakes. They had produced what has become the most popular ready-to-eat breakfast cereal in the world.

The original Kellogg's cornflakes packet.

What are breakfast cereals?

In Britain, many people now eat breakfast cereals instead of the traditional bacon and egg breakfast.

Grains, such as maize, wheat, and rice are cooked in water under pressure, then flaked, shredded, or puffed up to give different shapes when baked. The most popular breakfast cereals are cornflakes and wheat biscuits.

Breakfast cereals need to be eaten with milk to provide useful nutrients. Some cereals have added nutrients, and many are made from wholegrain cereals or bran and provide useful dietary fibre. Many cereals are already sweetened, so extra sugar should not be added.

Make your own muesli

A muesli base contains a mixture of processed grain, e.g. rolled oats and wheat flakes. Add some bran, sugar, and skimmed milk powder to this base, and then add whatever dried ingredients you fancy. Nuts, dried fruit, dates, and coconut can be added. Stir the mixture and store in a jar. Muesli can be eaten with milk, yoghurt, and fresh, chopped apple.

Questions
1 How is pasta made?
2 How were cornflakes invented?
3 What is the value of breakfast cereals in the diet?

Homework
1 Look at the information on a breakfast cereal packet.
   (a) Name the product and say which cereal it is made from.
   (b) What is the nutritional information given on the packet?
   (c) What has to be done to the product to make it ready for eating?
   (d) What other useful information is given on the packet?
2 Visit your local supermarket and find out:
   (a) What flours are sold there and how much they cost.
   (b) What different breakfast cereals are sold and what grains are used.
   (c) What different sorts of pasta are sold.
   (d) What other products made from cereals are sold.
3 Collect pictures of cereal products such as cakes and pastries, and label them to show what cereals they are made from.

Nearly 3000 years ago, the Persians discovered how to extract sugar from sugar cane, and they guarded their secret well. In England, in the 18th century, sugar was so expensive that it was called 'white gold', and the rich people who could afford sugar locked it away from their servants.

Sugar cane grows in countries like the West Indies because it needs a tropical climate. Wars in Europe made it very difficult to get the sugar cane from these countries. So Napoleon set his scientists the task of finding new ways to obtain sugar. Large areas were sown with sugar beet and the scientists found out how to extract the sugar from it. In Britain today, half our sugar comes from sugar beet.

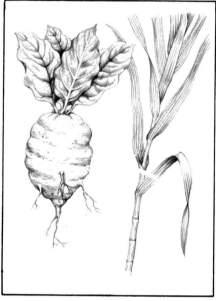

How is sugar made?

The cane or beet is chopped, crushed, and mixed with water to dissolve the sugar. This liquid is boiled to obtain the sugar crystals. White sugar needs to be cleaned or purified.

Sugar beet is like a long turnip and is pinky-white in colour. The sugar is found in the root.
Sugar cane looks like bamboo and the sugar is found in the stem.

Types of sugar

Granulated sugar is the most popular sugar. It is used to sweeten tea and coffee as well as fruit and breakfast cereals.
Caster sugar has smaller crystals, and is used in cake making and cooking.

Icing sugar is ground-up granulated sugar. It can be used for icings, sweets, and meringues.
Brown sugars have more flavour than white sugars, but they are no better for us than white sugar.

Black treacle and golden syrup are also sugar products.

How much sugar should we eat?

In Britain, each person eats nearly 350 g of sugar a *week*, compared with Elizabeth I's time when each person ate 450 g of sugar a *year*! Elizabeth's teeth were black, and a visitor said it was 'a defect the English seem subject to from their too great use of sugar'. Sugar contains carbohydrate and provides plenty of energy. A heaped teaspoon of sugar supplies about 30 Calories, the same as a small apple or half a slice of bread. However, sugar supplies 'empty Calories' because it contains no other nutrients.

Very few of us are short of Calories, so if we eat too much sugar, we are likely to get fat. Foods such as bread and rice are better sources of energy because they contain other nutrients as well.

Hidden sugar

Sugar is not only found in the sugar bowl. Obvious foods containing sugar include jams, cakes, sweets, biscuits, tinned fruit, and sweetened drinks. But many foods contain large amounts of hidden sugar. Even savoury foods such as beefburgers and baked beans can contain sugar.

Sugar and tooth decay

Sugar is the main cause of tooth decay. One third of all the people over sixteen in Britain do not have their own teeth. During the Second World War, when sugar was rationed, children's teeth needed fewer fillings.

It is not the quantity of sugar, but how often sugary foods are eaten which causes the most damage. If sweet foods are eaten throughout the day, the teeth are constantly surrounded by sugar. Sticky sweets and chocolates cause the greatest problem because they can get trapped in between the teeth.

Brushing the teeth after eating meals or sweets helps clean the teeth. Cheese and nuts are good teeth cleaners when it is not possible to use a toothbrush.

Questions

1 How is sugar made?
2 Give the names of *three* different types of sugar and suggest *two* uses for each.
3 What does the term 'empty Calories' mean when applied to sugar?
4 What health problems may be caused by eating too much sugar?

Homework

Visit a local supermarket. List the different sugars for sale, and find out the cost of each sugar. Name ten products which contain sugar.

FATS AND OILS

Our ancestors knew very few of the fats we use today. They may have been healthier because they ate less fat. Both plants and animals contain fat, and their fat can be used in different ways.

Butter
Butter is made by churning cream. Some people prefer the taste of butter, but others cannot tell it from margarine.

Suet
Large amounts of fat are found in beef and lamb animals, especially around the kidneys. This fat is grated and called suet, and can be used for pastries, mincemeat, and Christmas puddings.

Lard
Pig's fat is melted to become lard, which is almost a pure fat. It is used for frying and in pastry making. Cooking fat is made to look like lard, and comes from fats and oils.

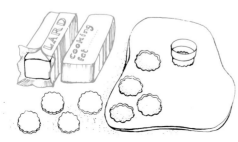

Dripping
Beef dripping is made by gently melting beef fat. It is used for roasting meat and potatoes. During the war, dripping on toast was called a 'nourishing snack', which it is not!

Oil
The best known cooking oil is olive oil, but oil can come from sunflower seeds, soya beans, and many other sources. Oil can fry food at high temperatures without burning. It is also used to make salad dressings.

Make your own oil
Since oil can be made from crushed nuts, try making your own. Put some peanuts or almonds in a strong polythene bag and crush them with a rolling pin to make a little oil. Use the crushed nuts in cakes or biscuits.

Margarine

Margarine was invented in France in 1869. Napoleon III asked his food chemist to make something which tasted like butter, but did not cost so much. The chemist used suet, chopped cow's udder, and a little warm milk, and made a rather waxy, pale fat, which he called margarine, after the Greek word for 'pearl', *margaron*.

Today, margarine can be made from animal or vegetable oils and fats. The oils are hardened by the addition of hydrogen gas. The more hydrogen gas that is added, the harder the fat becomes. Soft margarine contains less hydrogen.

Whey, from cheese-making, is used with salt to flavour the margarine. By law, margarine must contain 80% fat and no more than 16% water. Vitamins A and D must be added.

Margarine is no longer the 'poor man's butter'. It is just as nutritious – and just as fattening!

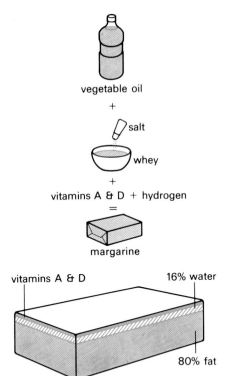

vegetable oil
+
salt
whey
+
vitamins A & D + hydrogen
=
margarine

vitamins A & D   16% water

80% fat

Composition of margarine

How to keep and use margarine

Soft margarines should be used straight from the fridge, as they become oily at room temperature. Margarine will keep in the fridge for three months.

Margarine is used for cakes and pastries. However, it is unwise to use it for frying, as it spits at high temperatures.

Low-fat spreads are nearly 50% water. These fats can be used to spread on bread, but they should not be used for frying, as their high water content makes them spit when heated.

Soft margarine spreads easily.

A low-fat spread.

Questions
1 Name *four* animal fats, and describe how they are made.
2 How is margarine made, and what vitamins are added to it?
3 What can oil be made from, and how is it used in cooking?

Homework
1 Find out the meanings of the sayings: 'butter fingers', 'butter would not melt in his mouth', and 'to butter one's bread on both sides'.
2 Visit a local supermarket and make a list of all the different types of fat and oil for sale. Compare their prices and say which come from animals and which come from plants.

FURTHER WORK

How well do you know your food?

For each question, answer either True or False. Check your answers on p. 115 and score one point for each correct answer.

1 If an egg floats in water it is fresh.
True or false?

2 Oily fish contain more fat than white fish.
True or false?
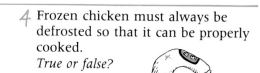

3 An egg contains all the food the growing chick needs.
True or false?

4 Frozen chicken must always be defrosted so that it can be properly cooked.
True or false?
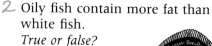

5 Custard powder is made from oats.
True or false?

6 Liver and kidney are rich in iron.
True or false?
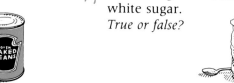

7 There is no goodness in white flour.
True or false?
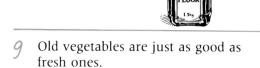

8 All meat should be thoroughly cooked.
True or false?

9 Old vegetables are just as good as fresh ones.
True or false?

10 An apple a day is better for you than an orange if you want plenty of vitamin C.
True or false?

11 Bacon is salted beef.
True or false?

12 All margarine comes from vegetable oil.
True or false?

13 There is no goodness in baked beans.
True or false?

14 Brown sugar is better for you than white sugar.
True or false?

Crossword

Across
1 Eggs of a fish (3)
2 A blue English cheese (7)
3 Ground to make flour (5)
4 Stale food has gone _____. (3)
5 Middle of the egg (4)
6 Eggs can be farmed by _____ litter. (4)
7 The outside of a grain of wheat (4)
8 Louis _____ discovered how to make milk safe. (7)

Down
2 A food forming the main part of the diet (6)
9 _____ fish contain fat in their flesh. (4)
10 A _____ lays eggs. (3)
11 The insides and trimmings from an animal (5)
12 The most popular English cheese (7)
13 Used to make porridge (4)
14 Used to make bread (5)

Top of the form

Each member of the group must write down two questions about food, with their answers. Extra questions are useful in case people choose the same questions. As each member asks their questions, the others write down their answers. At the end of questioning, the answers are given, and the winner is the person with the highest score. Extra questions may be used for a tie-breaker.

Homework

1 Make a list of the main foods in the 'shopping basket' which your family buys regularly, e.g. flour, sugar, rice, margarine, etc. Cost each item. Find out where each food comes from and how it is produced ready for sale. How is each food prepared for eating?

2 Draw a picture of a fridge. Show where the following fresh foods should be stored in it: cheese, fish, meat, cooked meat, milk, eggs, salad vegetables, butter, lard. How long should each of these foods be kept in the fridge before they are eaten, and what special storage wrapping, if any, does each of them need?

3 What nutrients are these foods good sources of: milk, flour, butter, sugar, margarine, fish, eggs, cheese, fruit, vegetables, meat, offal?

4 Food has given its name to many sayings. Find out what the following phrases mean: a red herring, a bean feast, a fish out of water, an egg head, a piece of cake, bring home the bacon, not my cup of tea.

4.IN THE KITCHEN

KITCHEN PLANNING

A kitchen is a very busy place. For example, it is used for preparing, cooking, and eating food, and for washing up.

Make a list of all the activities which take place in *your* kitchen.

A kitchen should be well planned to make it easy and safe to use. The main pieces of equipment in a kitchen are the **sink**, the **cooker**, and the **fridge**. It is important to think about the positioning of this equipment to avoid too much walking about.

Try this experiment in a kitchen you know, to see if the equipment is in the best position:
Prepare some instant potato by boiling some water in a saucepan, mixing it into the potato powder, and adding some margarine from the fridge. Clear away and wash up.
Write down the journeys you made. Draw a simple plan of your kitchen, and mark the path you took to collect the equipment, prepare the potato, and clear away. Suggest any changes which might improve the plan.

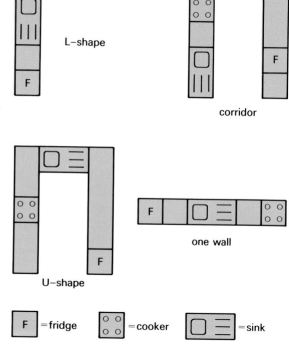

Shapes of kitchens

L-shape

corridor

U-shape

one wall

F = fridge   = cooker   = sink

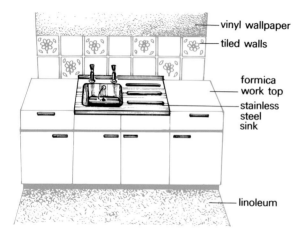

vinyl wallpaper

tiled walls

formica work top

stainless steel sink

linoleum

Materials in the kitchen

Kitchen surfaces are specially designed to be easily cleaned. Walls can be painted or tiled, or washable vinyl wallpaper can be used. Floors should be washable and non slip, and vinyl tiles or linoleum can be fitted. Work tops need to be hard-wearing. Plastics, like formica, can be used. The sink is often made of stainless steel, which does not chip and is easy to clean.

How high should the work tops and cupboards be?

It is important to use work tops which are the correct height for you. If they are too low, then they will be tiring to work on, and may give you backache. It is difficult to work on surfaces which are too high. Cupboards which are too high on the wall are dangerous, because you need to climb or stretch to take things out of them.

What is the correct height?

People are different heights, so find out your *own* working height. Remember that as you grow this working height will change. Stand in front of the work table and place your hands flat on the surface. If you are standing upright, with your arms straight, then this is your correct working height. Write down how tall you are, and record your working height.

working height

If you had to stoop or bend your elbows, then the height is wrong. Find a surface which is the correct height for you. Measure it and record it with your height.

Bad planning can cause accidents

Keep chairs and stools away from the cooking area.

A cooker needs a work surface next to it, to put hot pans on.

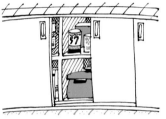

Keep the cooker away from opening doors. Sliding doors are safer on cupboards.

Good lighting and ventilation are important.

When in regular use, cupboards should be easy to reach.

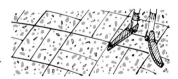

Choose non-slip floors and easy-to-clean surfaces.

Questions

1 Draw the four shapes of kitchen, and show where you would put important pieces of equipment.
2 Describe the different surfaces used in kitchens for (a) walls, (b) floors, (c) sinks, (d) work tops.

Homework

Imagine that you could design a kitchen of your choice. Draw a simple plan, and show where you would put the important equipment. Describe the colours you would choose for the walls, cupboards, and floors. What else would you like in this kitchen? 77

The cooker

When choosing a cooker, think about:

1 **Price** How much money do you have to spend? Buy only what you can afford. Ask friends or read magazines to find the 'best buy'.
2 **Size** Make sure the cooker fits the space in the kitchen. Think about the number of people to be cooked for.
3 **Cleaning** Choose a cooker which is easy to clean. Some cookers have special linings in the oven which burn off food and keep themselves clean.
4 **Gadgets and fitments** The grill can have different positions. An eye-level grill is easy to see and safer if there are children around. Extra gadgets cost money. Decide whether you need all the extras.

Find the leaflet for the cooker you use. Draw the cooker, and label the grill, hob, and oven. Find out how they work. Describe any gadgets or special features of the cooker, and find out how to use them.

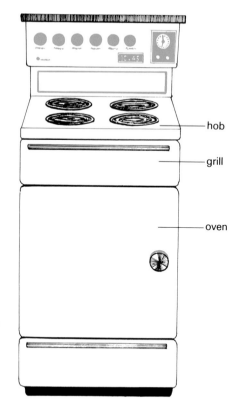

hob

grill

oven

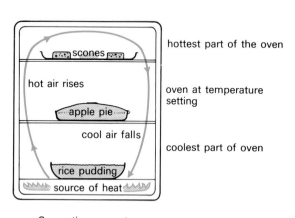

hottest part of the oven

oven at temperature setting

coolest part of oven

Convection currents

How does an oven work?

An oven is a well-sealed box, heated by gas, electricity, or solid fuel. As the air is heated, it rises to the top of the oven, then falls as it cools. These movements of air are called **convection currents**. Convection currents make the oven hotter at the top and cooler at the bottom. These 'zones of heat' mean that dishes which need to be cooked at different heats can be cooked at the same time. Some ovens have a fan which makes all parts of the oven the same temperature.

Experiment

Use an electric oven with an autotimer. Switch the oven on to 200°C, 400°F. A red light shows that the oven is not at the correct temperature. How long does it take for the light to go out, and for the oven to reach the temperature setting? Write this information down for later use.

78

Food mixers and liquidizers

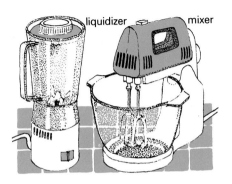

Some food mixers are held in the hand, and others are fixed to a heavy stand. Different beaters can be used for whisking food and making bread, pastry, and cakes. A liquidizer can churn chunky food such as fruit and vegetables into a liquid. Smooth soups and fruit purées can be made. Dry ingredients such as breadcrumbs and parsley can be chopped in a liquidizer.

Pressure cookers

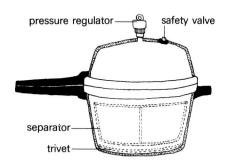

A pressure cooker is a heavy saucepan with a tight-sealing lid. When the liquid inside the cooker boils, the steam produced cannot escape. This trapped steam increases the pressure inside the cooker and raises the temperature of the boiling liquid, so water inside a pressure cooker can boil at 110–120°C instead of 100°C. Food will cook faster at these high temperatures.

Microwave ovens

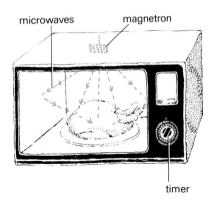

Food cooks very quickly in a microwave oven – a baked potato takes only four minutes to cook in a microwave oven, when it could take an hour in an ordinary oven. The microwaves are produced by the magnetron in the oven. They bounce off the metal sides of the oven and beam on to the food. The energy from the microwaves passes into the food and makes it hot, but the oven itself remains cold. Food cooked by microwaves does not turn brown on the outside.

Questions
1 List three points which should be considered when buying a cooker.
2 Describe how an oven heats up food.
3 What is meant by 'zones of heat'?
4 How does a pressure cooker cook food quickly?
5 How does a microwave oven cook food?

Homework
1 List four small pieces of equipment and gadgets used in the kitchen. Describe how each of these is useful to the cook.
2 Imagine that you live in a bedsit. What pieces of equipment would you buy to help you with the cooking? Describe how you could cook a meal in the room.
3 Plan *two* three-course meals, one of which can be cooked entirely on the hob, and the other to be cooked entirely in the oven.

Fridges

Food will stay fresh longer when it is kept cool. Older houses were often built with cool, dry larders where food could be kept. Modern kitchens rarely have the space for a larder, and a 'refrigerator' or 'fridge' is used to keep food cool. The temperature inside a fridge is about 5°C, so the bacteria which can spoil food (see p. 88) are too cold to be very active.

How does a fridge work?

The rule of science which helps a fridge to work is: *Hot air rises and cold air sinks.*

The icebox or freezer compartment produces cold air which falls to the bottom of the fridge, cooling the food it passes. The air becomes warmer and rises. These air movements are called **convection currents**.

Moving air can draw the water out of food. This water collects around the icebox as ice. Uncovered food dries out, and liquids evaporate unless they are covered. If the fridge is packed tightly with food, the air cannot move around, and so the air in the fridge will not be properly cooled.

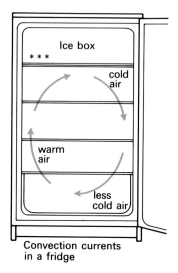

Convection currents in a fridge

Fridge rules

1 **Star markings** on the icebox show the recommended storage time for frozen food.
   * = 1 week   ** = 1 month
   *** = 3 months

2 Store meat and fish at the top of the fridge where it is coldest.

3 All food should be covered and wrapped if it is to remain moist.

4 Strong-smelling foods should be stored in airtight containers.

5 Do not overpack the fridge.

6 Open the door as little as possible to prevent warm air entering.

7 Salad vegetables must be covered and stored at the bottom of the fridge.

8 Hot food should be cooled before it is placed in the fridge, to keep the temperature low.

How to defrost and clean a fridge

Defrost the fridge when the ice around the icebox is 5 mm thick. If the ice is too thick, the fridge will not work properly.

There are three ways that fridges can be defrosted:

Automatic The fridge defrosts itself as it works.

Semi-automatic The fridge defrosts when a button is pressed, and restarts after defrosting is completed.

Manual Switch off the fridge, remove the food and store it in a cool place. Put a bowl of hot water under the icebox, leave the fridge door open and let the ice melt into the bowl. Clean the inside of the fridge with bicarbonate of soda and water, because soapy water might flavour the food. Dry out the inside, switch on and replace the food.

Freezers

Frozen food is stored at −18°C in a freezer. The food will not go bad in these conditions because it is too cold for the bacteria, yeasts, and moulds to work. If frozen food is stored and wrapped correctly, then when it is thawed, it will be as pleasant as when it was fresh. There are three main types of freezer:

Chest freezers

These need more floor space than upright freezers, but by having a lid on top, less cold air escapes when it is opened. Short people sometimes find it difficult to reach packs at the bottom.

Upright freezers

Less floor space is needed for these freezers, and the contents can be easily seen. Cold air can escape when the door is opened.

Fridge-freezers

The fridge and the freezer are contained in one cabinet, and work together from one motor. This may be more convenient for a smaller family.

Looking after a freezer

Defrost the freezer once or twice a year. Clean out the inside of the cabinet with bicarbonate of soda and water and then dry.

Fridge-freezer.

Questions

1 Why is it best to leave the tops on milk bottles when they are in the fridge?
2 Hot jelly should not be cooled in a fridge. Why?
3 Chopped onion must be stored in an airtight container in a fridge. Why?
4 Why should a fridge not be overpacked?
5 Why must a fridge be defrosted when the icebox has more than 5 mm of ice on it?

Homework

Collect leaflets and pictures of different sorts of fridges and freezers from shops or magazines. Choose the fridge and the freezer which you like best and describe why you like them.

KITCHEN EQUIPMENT (3)

The chart shows some basic kitchen tools. You may like to add some ideas of your own.

Equipment	Uses	Equipment	Uses
1 wooden spoon	stirring and mixing food 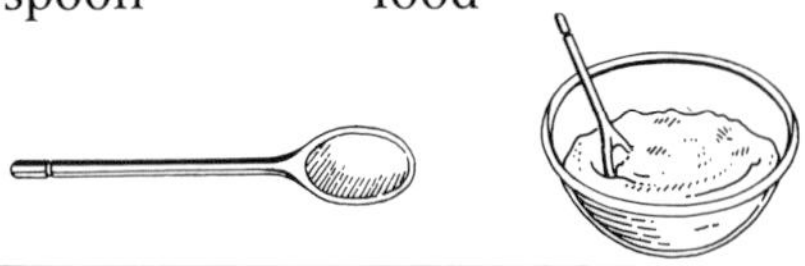	2 paring knife	peeling fruit and vegetables 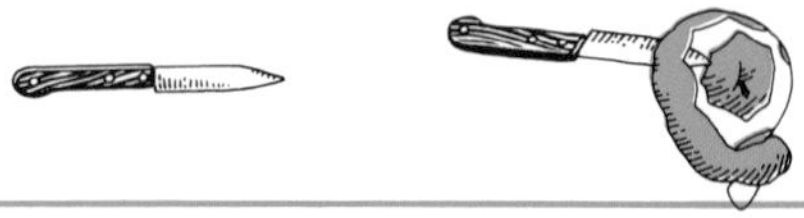
3 tablespoon	measuring, stirring, and serving food	4 balloon whisk rotary whisk	beating and whisking food 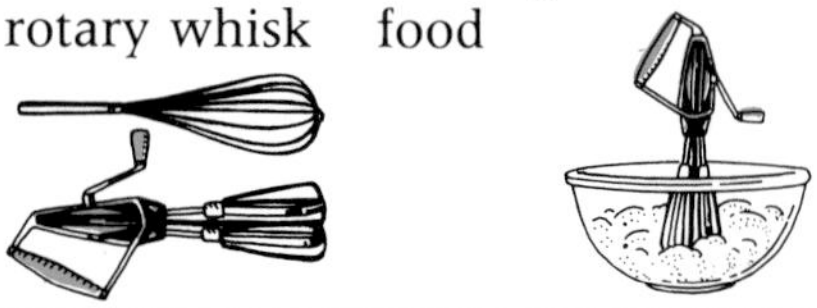
5 dessertspoon	measuring ingredients and eating food 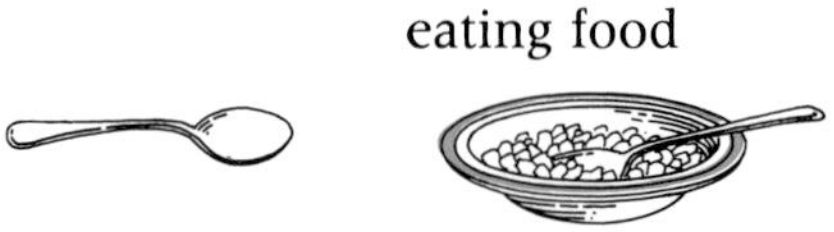	6 fork	mixing, mashing, and eating food 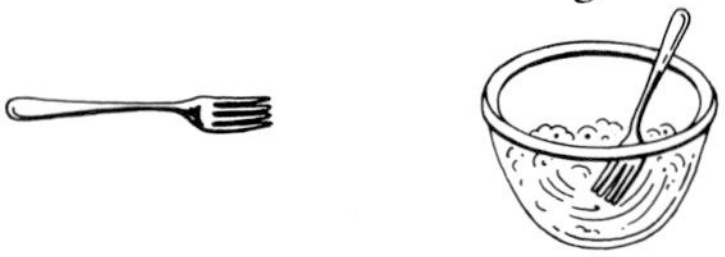
7 teaspoon	small measurements, eating food	8 spatula	scraping mixtures from bowls 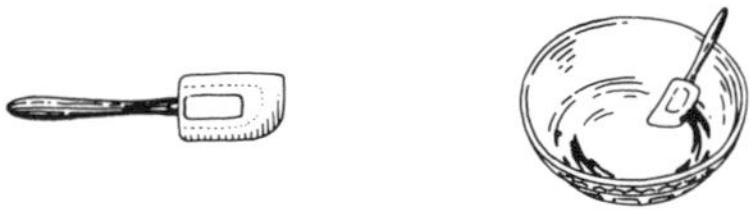
9 palette knife	lifting and mixing food 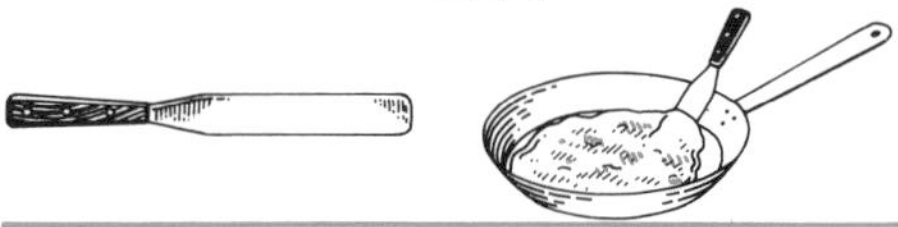	10 rolling pin	rolling out pastry 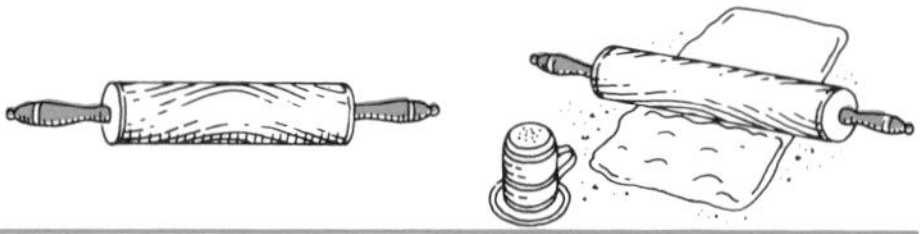
11 cook's knife	chopping and cutting 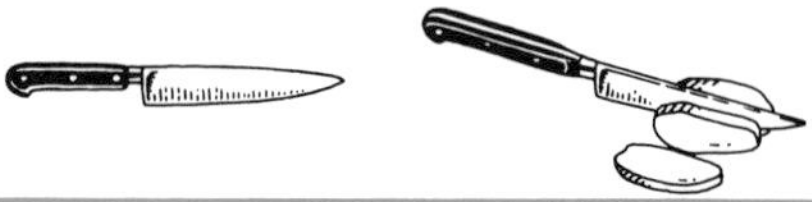	12 pastry brush	brushing glazes on to pastry 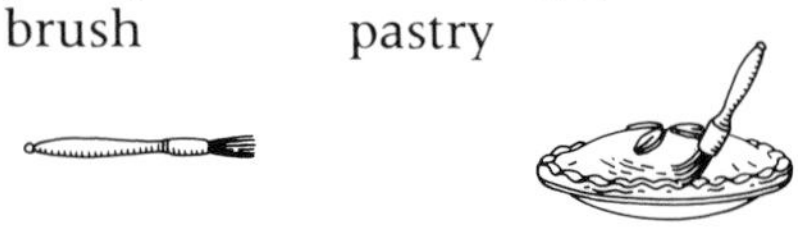
13 serrated knife	cutting fruit and vegetables 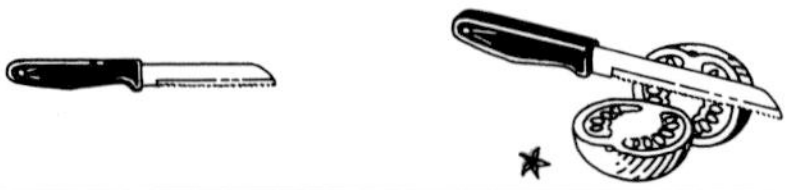	14 vegetable peeler	peeling vegetables 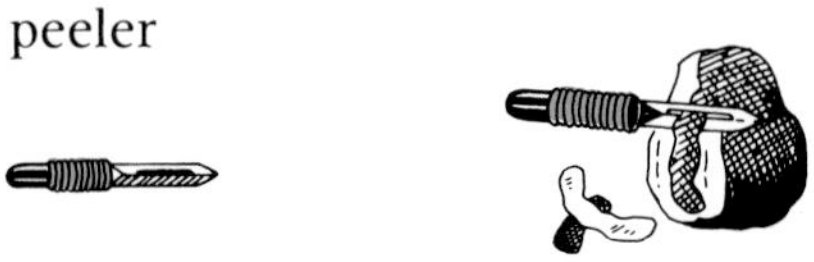

This chart shows important equipment needed for simple food preparation:

Equipment	Use	Equipment	Use
1 baking tray, cake tins	placing things in the oven; cooking cakes in	2 grater	grating cheese
3 mixing bowls	mixing ingredients in	4 measuring jug	measuring liquids
5 chopping board	cutting and preparing meat and vegetables on	6 cooling rack	cooling cakes and biscuits
7 sieve colander	sieving flour draining vegetables	8 frying pan saucepan	frying food boiling food

Draw this chart. Write in one more use for each piece of equipment. Include two more pieces of equipment that you think are useful.

Which kitchen tool is best for the job?

1 Select three clean potatoes of the same weight. Collect a cook's knife, a paring knife, and a vegetable peeler. Peel each of the potatoes using a different tool. Weigh the amount of peel from each potato separately. Describe which tool was the best choice for this job, and why.

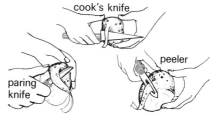

2 Put the whites of three eggs into three bowls, labelled A, B, and C. Use an electric whisk with bowl A, a rotary or balloon whisk with bowl B, and a fork with bowl C. Whisk the egg whites until they are stiff enough to remain in the bowl even when it is turned upside down. Measure the time each tool takes and describe which was the best choice for the job, and why.

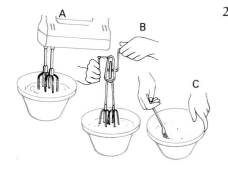

Every day in the UK, fifteen people die as a result of accidents in the home. Many of these are children and old people. Accidents are often caused by carelessness.

Burns and scalds – 50 deaths every year

Burns can be caused by fire, flames, or hot objects. A gas flame could set tea-towels, oven gloves and even curtains alight. Keep children away from the cooker when in use.

Scalds are caused by boiling water, steam, or hot oil. Keep saucepan handles and electric kettles out of children's reach. Chip pans can catch fire and the oil can scald.

Cuts – 25 deaths every year

Never leave sharp knives or pointed equipment lying around, especially where children might reach them. Do not walk about with sharp knives.

Falls – 3000 deaths every year

Use non-slip flooring in the kitchen. Mop up puddles of fat and water. Keep children, toys, and stools out of the working area.

Poisoning – 600 deaths every year

Store medicines and cleaning materials, especially bleach, out of children's reach. Keep household chemicals in their own bottles. *Never* put them in lemonade bottles.

Electrocution – 65 deaths every year

Water conducts electricity, so never touch switches with wet hands. Keep plugs and flexes in good condition.

First aid kit

A first aid kit is useful for dealing with small injuries or helping someone who has had an accident before medical help arrives.

First aid materials should be kept handy in a box.

plasters for covering small cuts

triangular bandage to make slings

scissors and safety pins for cutting and doing up bandages

stretch bandage for bandaging sprains

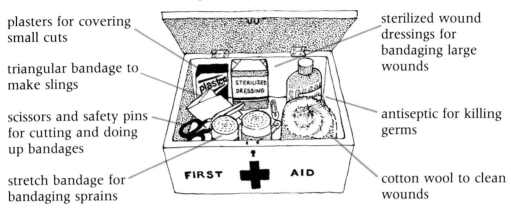

sterilized wound dressings for bandaging large wounds

antiseptic for killing germs

cotton wool to clean wounds

Accidents happen quickly, and it is important to know what to do. If the accident is serious, call 999 and ask for an ambulance, or ring for a doctor.

Simple first aid

Cuts
Clean small cuts with running water. Dry the skin with cotton wool and cover with a plaster.

For large cuts, try and stop the bleeding by pressing on the wound. Call for medical help.

Electrocution
Switch off at the mains, and only then attend to the casualty. Reassure the patient and get medical help.

Burns and scalds
Soak the burn in plenty of cold water and leave for ten minutes, or until the pain goes. If clothing catches fire, smother the flames by covering with rugs or towels.

Cover the burn with a *dry* dressing. Never rub in fat or lotion.

For large or severe burns call for medical help immediately.

Poisoning
Find out what has been taken. Telephone the doctor and follow her instructions.

Questions
1 A child's clothing has caught fire from a flaming chip pan. What should you do?
2 A baby is lying on the floor holding an empty bottle of household bleach. What should you do?
3 Your grandmother has tipped a teapot full of hot tea over her hand. What should you do?
4 Name three important items in a first aid box, and describe what each is used for.
5 Describe two minor accidents which could happen in the kitchen, and say how you would treat them.

Homework
Design a poster with the title: 'Safety in the kitchen'.

Clean work surfaces regularly.

All food in the cupboard should be covered.

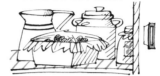

Waste bins should be emptied as soon as they are full. Wash them out regularly.

Dustbins should be stored away from the kitchen, and have a tight-fitting lid.

Dishcloths and tea-towels should be washed frequently. Boiling or bleach will kill bacteria.

The sink and drains should be disinfected once a week.

Sweep up crumbs and mop up spilled food quickly. Food scraps encourage pests.

Pets and tiny children should not be allowed in the kitchen.

Sweep and wash the kitchen floor regularly.

Keep soap, nailbrush, and towel beside the sink for washing hands.

Clean and wipe out the fridge regularly, and throw away stale food.

Make sure that equipment is clean before you store it.

The most important rule is: **Keep food clean, cool, and covered.**

Pests in the kitchen

Pests spread disease. They eat uncovered food and food scraps, so clear all food away. Deal with pests quickly or they will increase in number!

Flies visit rubbish dumps and rotting food, and pick up decaying matter on the sticky cushions on their feet. They pass food-poisoning bacteria on to food.

Mice and rats pass on food-poisoning bacteria from the dirty places they visit. We might eat food they have chewed or left their droppings on.

Personal hygiene in the kitchen

1 Dangerous bacteria can grow in the nose and throat, and can be passed to food.

Do not cough or spit over food.
Do not smoke near food.

Do not wipe your nose and then handle food. Paper hankies must be thrown away.

Do not lick your fingers during food preparation. Taste food with a clean teaspoon.

2 Cuts and sores on the skin are breeding grounds for bacteria. Dangerous bacteria are passed out with the faeces.

Cover all cuts and sores with waterproof dressings.

Always wash your hands well after visiting the toilet.

3 Bacteria are found on the hair, skin, and nails.

Always wash your hands before handling food.

Keep nails short and clean.

Tie your hair back and do not touch your face or hair during food preparation.

4 Clothing, cleaning cloths, and surfaces can all pass on bacteria.

Cover your clothes with an apron or overall before starting to cook. Then wash your hands.

Wipe down the work surfaces before you use them.

Use clean tea-towels and dishcloths, and wash them after use.

Questions
1 How do flies and mice pass food-poisoning bacteria on to food?
2 Why is it important to (a) wash your hands after visiting the toilet, (b) cover cuts and sores, (c) cover clothes before cooking?
3 Why should food be tasted with a *clean* teaspoon?

Homework
Look at the information on these pages, and make a list, under the heading: 'My ten rules of good kitchen hygiene'.

Our food comes from plants and animals. Once they have been harvested or killed, changes take place. In time, food spoils, or goes 'bad'. If this food is eaten, it can cause food poisoning and illness.

Food spoilage is caused by micro-organisms which are too small to be seen with the naked eye, but which can be seen through a microscope. Micro-organisms are found everywhere – in water, dust, on food, and on the hands. There are three types of micro-organism which cause food spoilage. They are: **yeast, mould,** and **bacteria.**

Yeasts Yeasts need food, warmth, and liquid to grow rapidly. They use the sugar in food to grow and produce carbon dioxide gas and alcohol. They are killed at high temperatures. Yeasts can be useful. They help bread to rise, and make wines and beers by a process called **fermentation**. But yeasts may attack fruits and jams and spoil them.

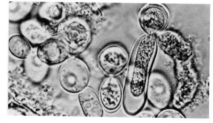
Yeast cells budding.

Mould.

Mould You have probably seen mouldy bread. Mould spores are carried in the air and can settle and grow on food such as bread, cheese, and meat. They grow fastest on moist food and will even grow in the fridge. Moulds are killed by heat. We deliberately eat some mouldy foods, such as blue cheese.

Bacteria Bacteria are the most commonly found of the three types of micro-organism. Some bacteria are useful, some just spoil the food, but others cause an illness called **food poisoning** (pp. 90–91). Bacteria are killed by boiling, but food-poisoning bacteria can produce spores and poisons which can survive twenty mintues or longer in a boiling liquid.

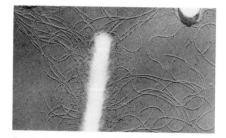
Bacterium magnified 20,000 times.

Enzymes cause apples to turn brown.

Changes in food can also be caused by enzymes. Enzymes are chemicals in food which cause chemical changes. When apples turn brown, this is a chemical change. Enzymes are destroyed by heat. If air and water are removed, then most enzymes cannot work.

Experiments to show the action of bacteria, moulds, and enzymes

Bacteria
Yoghurt is made by the action of bacteria. Turn to page 47 to find out how to make your own yoghurt. Colonies of bacteria can be grown on agar jelly. For instructions for this experiment turn to page 91.

Mould
Mould is found on food and in the air. Try growing your own mould. Leave some moist bread and cheese loosely wrapped in a clear polythene bag. Look at the food after a few days to see if there is mould growth. Flick the bag to release the mould spores. Throw the bag and contents away without opening them.

Enzymes
Rennet is made from the enzyme **rennin**. Rennet sets junket, a pudding which looks like a milk jelly.

To make junket
Warm 500 ml of milk with 10 g sugar to blood heat. Test by dipping a finger in the milk. When it feels warm, this is blood heat. Pour the milk into a serving dish, stir in a teaspoon of rennet, and leave to set for $1\frac{1}{2}$–2 hours. Chill in the fridge before serving. Rennin is a body enzyme which works at body heat, and this is why the milk must be warm. Try making junket with boiling milk. What happens?

The story of sourdough, the wilderness yeast

Some 4000 years before Christ, the Egyptians discovered that when flour and water are left together in the warmth, they begin to bubble. This bubbling, called **fermentation**, is caused by wild yeasts attacking the dough. When baked, this dough produces a light, risen bread.

In North America the early gold prospectors carried a sourdough pot on their travels. The sourdough was made from wild yeasts, flour, and water. It was used for raising bread, cakes, and pancakes. There is a story about an old prospector who lost his mule and sourdough in a snowslide. So precious was the sourdough, that he climbed down and scraped some off the dead animal. He knew he could not cook his bread without the sourdough.

Questions
1 Name the three micro-organisms which cause food spoilage. Describe how *one* causes food spoilage, and say how it can be destroyed.
2 What are enzymes? How do they affect food and how can they be destroyed?
3 Name the enzyme used to make junket, and describe how junket is made.

Homework
Describe ways in which yeast is used to make different foods and drinks.

FOOD POISONING

Bacteria are everywhere – in the air, soil, water, and dust. Some bacteria are useful, but others are dangerous because they cause disease. Food-poisoning bacteria can cause illness two hours or as long as forty-eight hours after poisoned food is eaten. Bacteria are so small that they can only be seen with a microscope. They cannot be seen on food and the food may not even taste bad, yet bacteria and their poisons could still be present in large numbers. The victim suffers from stomach pains, diarrhoea, and sickness which can last one or two days, or even longer. One type of food poisoning can cause death.

There are three conditions which these bacteria need to live and breed: **food, warmth,** and **moisture.**

Every twenty or thirty minutes, a bacterium can divide in two.

Work out this puzzle: If a piece of meat containing two bacteria is left in a warm room and the bacteria divide in two every twenty minutes, how many bacteria will there be at the end of four hours?

How food poisoning is carried

1 Bacteria are found in the nose, throat, and sores on the skin, as well as in the faeces. We can pass the bacteria from these places on to the food we prepare. Hands must be washed after visiting the toilet.

2 Pests and pets pass bacteria on to the food we eat.

3 Food such as raw chicken or meat may contain food-poisoning bacteria. After touching these foods, the hands can pass bacteria on to other foods.

4 Surfaces and equipment can harbour bacteria. If dirty dishcloths are wiped over surfaces, they can spread bacteria. A dirty meat slicer could infect other meat.

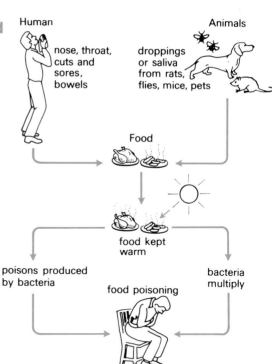

Human
nose, throat, cuts and sores, bowels

Animals
droppings or saliva from rats, flies, mice, pets

Food

food kept warm

poisons produced by bacteria

food poisoning

bacteria multiply

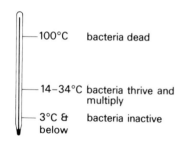

100°C — bacteria dead

14–34°C — bacteria thrive and multiply

3°C & below — bacteria inactive

Where bacteria live

Bacteria thrive on nutritious food which is not too salty, sweet, or acid. They like warm, moist places, and multiply rapidly if undisturbed. Bacteria are killed by boiling, but some of their spores or poisons can survive twenty minutes' boiling. In the cold of the fridge or freezer they are inactive or 'dormant'.

An experiment to grow colonies of bacteria

Warning: This experiment is dangerous, since large numbers of bacteria may be grown. Only carry out this experiment if an adult is in charge, and use a science laboratory and *not* an area where food is prepared. The adult must dispose of the Petri dishes afterwards.

Method: Pour some Agar jelly into six sterilized Petri dishes, and leave to set. Infect five of the dishes with dirty objects, and leave one untouched as a control.

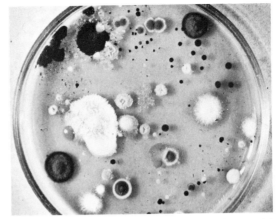

A variety of colonies of bacteria are growing on this Petri dish.

Here are some ideas for infecting the dishes: hands, hair, dishcloths, cough, handkerchief. Label, cover, and seal the dishes. Leave for up to one week in a warm place. Do not open the dishes, but draw and describe the results you can see. The control should be unchanged.

HAM POISONS COACH PARTY

Disaster struck a London coach party outing, on a trip to the seaside. Tucking into their ham sandwiches, they were unaware that they would all be rushed to hospital at the end of their journey.

WHAT HAPPENED

Health inspectors discovered that the sandwiches, prepared at the local pub, were poisoned. Food-poisoning bacteria had been passed from the cook's dirty hands on to the ham. The ham had then been stored in a warm room where the bacteria had multiplied to a dangerous poisonous level.

Food Poisoning reported on a coach tour . . .

The cook did not understand the basic rules of hygiene and food storage. Make a list of *five* rules which could be displayed in the kitchen to help with food hygiene.

Questions

1 How could the following situations lead to food poisoning: an uncovered cut on a finger, mice in the kitchen, a cook with a cough?
2 In what conditions do bacteria multiply most rapidly? What happens when they are boiled? What happens when they are frozen?

Homework

Write your own account of an outbreak of food poisoning – either real or imaginary. 91

PRESERVATION (1)

The micro-organisms **bacteria, yeast,** and **mould** cause food to go bad. **Enzymes** cause chemical changes in food.

Why does preservation stop food from going bad?

Micro-organisms need **food, warmth,** and **moisture** to multiply. If one of these conditions is taken away, the micro-organisms do not multiply and the food does not go bad.

The history of preservation

In countries like Britain, food is plentiful in the summer, but in the winter, little grows. Our ancestors had to find methods of preservation to stop food going bad during the long winter months. Many of their ways of preserving food are still used today.

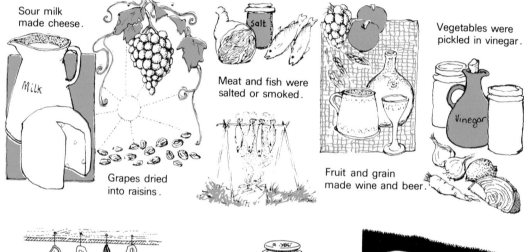

Sour milk made cheese.

Grapes dried into raisins.

Meat and fish were salted or smoked.

Fruit and grain made wine and beer.

Vegetables were pickled in vinegar.

By the Middle Ages, fruit and vegetables were dried in the sun.

With the introduction of sugar, jams and jellies could be made.

By the eighteenth century, wealthy homes owned icepits and ice houses in which food was kept cold.

Dry your own fruit

This 'fruit leather' makes a chewy snack.

Ingredients: one kilo apples, 50 g sugar *or* 2 tablespoons honey.

1 Line two baking trays with cling wrap and tape the edges.
2 Wash, core, and quarter the apples, but do not peel them.
3 Place the apple in a liquidizer and blend until the apple becomes a paste or purée. A little water may make this easier.

4 Add sugar or honey if the apples are sour.
5 Spread the purée over the baking trays and dry the apple.
   (a) *Sun dry* – leave the trays in the hot sun for two to three days.
   (b) *Oven dry* – 110°C, 225°F, Gas $\frac{1}{4}$. Leave the oven door slightly open, and let
   the apple dry for six hours or more until it feels like leather.
6 Roll up in the cling wrap and keep in a dry jar for up to two months.

Why does dried, salted, and smoked food keep for a long time?
Dried food does not contain enough water for the micro-organisms to multiply.
Salted and smoked food contains chemicals which kill micro-organisms.

The history of canning

In 1809, in France, Napoleon was at war and
needed help to find new ways of preserving
food to send to his soldiers. A chef called
Nicholas Appert discovered that when food
was heated in glass jars, then sealed to make
the jars airtight, the food would keep for
some time. Napoleon rewarded him for this
idea with a prize of 12,000 francs.

The English copied Appert's idea, but used
a tin canister as a container for the food. The
first canning factory probably opened in
Bermondsey, London, in 1812. Canned food
reached the shops in 1830, but was very
expensive. A kilo of corned beef cost $8\frac{1}{2}$ p,
when the weekly rent of a house was $12\frac{1}{2}$ p.

In modern factories today, a similar
canning method is used. Food is placed in
the cans, with hot liquid. The cans are
heated, sealed, and then heated again to
sterilize them. Canned food will keep for
long periods if the cans are not opened.

Inside a modern canning factory.
These cans will be filled with baked
beans.

Bottling

Fruit can be bottled at home by heating fruit
and liquid in glass jars to sterilize them, and
then covering them with an airtight seal.

**Why does canned and bottled food keep for
a long time?**
When the can or bottle of food is heated, the
micro-organisms are killed. The airtight seal
prevents any other micro-organisms from
entering and attacking the food.

Questions
1 Imagine that you lived four hundred years ago. Describe how you would have
   preserved food to make sure your family had enough food for the winter.
2 Describe how food is canned and bottled. Why does this food not go bad?

PRESERVATION (2)

Freezing and quick freezing

For thousands of years, snow and ice have been used during the winter months to keep food fresh. The first refrigerator was invented in the 1830s.

When food is frozen slowly, large ice crystals form inside. When the food is defrosted, these crystals break down the food and make it soft.

An American inventor, called Clarence Birdseye, discovered 'quick freezing'. On a hunting trip, he ate some fish which had been quickly frozen outdoors in very cold weather. He noticed how tender and fresh the fish was, and on returning home, he set about inventing a machine which could freeze foods at very low temperatures. When food is quick-frozen, smaller ice crystals are formed, which cause less damage to the food when it is defrosted.

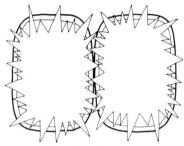

Slow freezing produces large ice crystals.

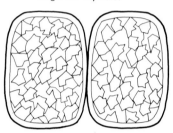

Quick freezing produces smaller ice crystals.

A freeze-drying cabinet.

Drying

For hundreds of years, fruit, vegetables, and even fish have been dried in the sun. When heat dries the food, it can change its flavour and shape. A new, better method has been invented called 'freeze drying'. The food is first frozen, then heated in a vacuum to drive off the ice. The ice is driven off as water vapour. This method of drying causes little damage to the food, and few nutrients are lost.

Why does frozen food stay fresh?

Frozen food is too cold for micro-organisms to grow. Most micro-organisms remain dormant in frozen food (see p. 90).

Peas are frozen in a freezing tunnel.

Is there any goodness left in preserved food?

People sometimes think that frozen, canned, and dried foods are not very nutritious. Some preserved food has, in fact, almost the same food value as fresh food. These days, 'fresh' fruit and vegetables can be several weeks old.

Canned fruit and vegetables have lost some of their vitamin C, but the vegetables are canned a few hours after picking and so may contain as much vitamin C as the fresh vegetables that have been cooked at home.

Frozen fruit and vegetables are likely to contain as much vitamin C as the fresh food. They are frozen quickly after harvesting and lose little vitamin C during freezing.

Freeze-dried vegetables are often as nutritious as fresh vegetables, but slow drying methods lead to loss of nutrients.

Records

In 1824, some canned food was put ashore from a ship in the Arctic. An expedition, led by Captain Ross, picked up the cans in 1829. One of Captain Ross's descendants opened the can in 1958 and found that the contents were still well preserved.

Should a tin can be called a tin or a can?
Tin can comes from the words tin canister. 'Can' is the correct term to use. 'Canister' comes from a Greek word meaning 'a basket to carry food in'.

Questions

1 List the different ways of preserving (a) plums, and (b) meat.
2 Copy out this paragraph and fill in the missing words:
  The three micro-organisms which make food go bad are y_____, m_____, and
  b_____. E_____ cause chemical changes in food. All these are killed by
  h_____. Frozen food is too c_____ for micro-organisms to grow. Dried food has
  too little w_____ in it, and canned food has killed the micro-organisms by
  h_____, and sealed the food to stop them getting in.
3 What is meant by the following terms: (a) quick freezing, (b) freeze drying?

Homework

1 Visit your local supermarket. Look around the shelves and list the different ways in which food is preserved. What sorts of food have been freeze-dried?

2 Start a project on 'preserving food at home'. Write about how to freeze, dry, and salt food. Find out how to make jams, jellies, chutneys, and pickles, and describe your favourite recipes.

3 Make a list of all the food you have eaten during the last three days. Underline foods which were dried, canned, or frozen. How would you change your eating habits if quick-freezing and canning had not been invented?

The kitchen can be the most dangerous room in the house.
Look at the picture, and make a list of:
(a) danger areas which could cause accidents
(b) poor hygiene which could lead to infected food.
How could this kitchen be made into a safer, cleaner place?

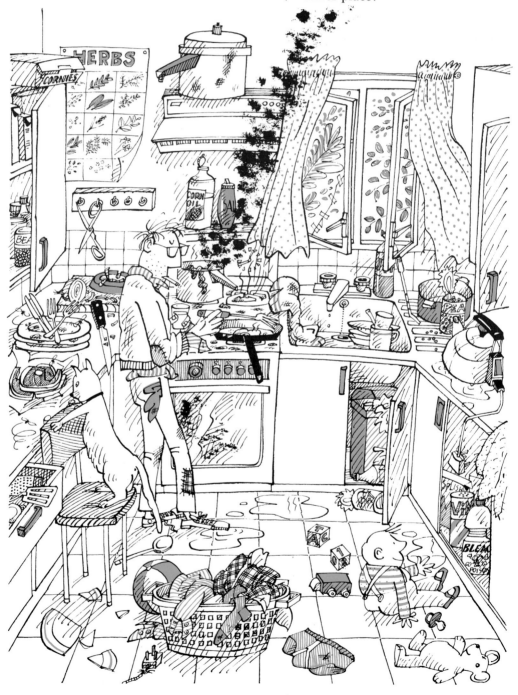

Safety crossword

Across
1 Do not touch these with wet hands. (8)
4 Fat and water on the floor may cause a _____. (4)
5 Butter or fat should never be rubbed onto a _____ on the skin. (4)
6 A sharp knife could cause this. (3)

Down
2 You would get this if you poured boiling water on your hands. (5)
3 Do not s_____ up to reach things from high cupboards. (7)
4 Fat in a hot chip pan could catch _____. (4)

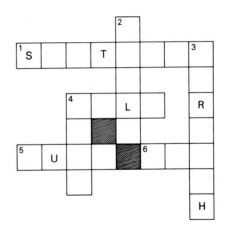

Food spoilage quiz

Find the word in the green box.
1 These cause food poisoning. (8)
2 These grow on damp bread. (6)
3 These make food ferment. 6)
4 Micro-organisms like to have food, moisture and _____. (6)
  These are chemicals which change food. (7)
The clue to the hidden word is: Food should be cool, covered, and _____.

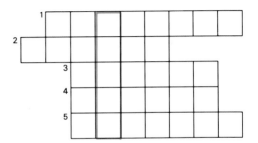

Homework

1 Start a project on kitchen equipment. Collect pictures from magazines, mail order catalogues, and shops to illustrate your project. Here are some ideas for you to use:
(a) Find out about different sorts of kitchen knives and their uses.
(b) Describe new equipment and gadgets and explain how they work.
(c) Draw some of the unusual tools in your own kitchen and explain how to use them.
(d) Ask an older person to explain how a cooker has changed over the years.

2 Find out about the work done by Environmental Health Officers. They can be contacted at the Town Hall, and may offer you leaflets or even give you a talk about the work they do.

3 Conduct a survey to see how clean your local food shops are. Look at the way the assistants are dressed for work. Notice their hands, nails, and hair. Do they use tongs to handle the food? Is the food kept clean before sale? Write a paragraph describing what you have seen.

4 (a) Choose three kitchen tools and three pieces of equipment. Describe a dish which could be prepared using all six items.
(b) Some small equipment can be replaced by using other tools. What could be used to replace the following: a rolling pin, a rotary whisk, a cooling rack, a large cake tin, a pastry brush, a spatula?

5. STARTING TO COOK

GETTING READY TO COOK

Before beginning to cook, make a clean start. Here are six simple rules:

1 Remove outdoor clothing and store bags and clothing out of the way, before entering the cooking area.
2 Cover clothing with a clean apron or overall.
3 Tie back long hair.
4 Wash your hands and dry them on a towel.
5 Collect clean tea-towels and dishcloths.
6 Wipe down the work surface before you begin to cook.

You are now ready to begin cooking. There are three important points to remember for good results:

Choose a good recipe book with clear instructions.

Turn on the oven if necessary.

Weigh out the ingredients accurately.

Good recipes have been tested by other cooks to make sure they work. Always read a recipe right through, and check that you have all the ingredients and equipment that you need before you start.

If you are using the oven, switch it on before you start cooking, so that it will have reached the correct temperature required to cook the dish. Sometimes the recipe says 'cook in a hot oven'. The chart on p. 115 shows the settings for gas and electric ovens, and the dishes which can be cooked at these settings.

While the oven is still cool, check that the shelves are in the correct position. Always use thick oven gloves to remove hot dishes from the oven.

Weighing and measuring

It is very important to weigh ingredients accurately. A dish could be spoilt by using the wrong amounts of ingredients.

Scales are used to weigh ingredients. If a **balancing scale** is used, then the scale pans and the weights should be level. If one side is higher than the other, then the measurement is incorrect.

Spring-balance scales show the weight of the ingredients on a dial.

Food can be weighed in grams, and there are 1000 grams (g) in a kilogram (kg).

Spoons can be used to measure food.

a tablespoon   *a dessertspoon*   *a teaspoon*

If you want a *level spoon*, heap the spoon with whatever you are measuring, and level it off with a knife.

A *heaped spoon* has the same amount of food above the spoon as in the bowl of the spoon.

Measuring jugs are used for measuring liquids. Liquids are measured in millilitres and litres. There are 1000 millilitres (ml) in a litre (l).

Measuring experiments

1 Use scales to find the weight of a level and a heaped tablespoon of:
   (a) flour, (b) sugar, (c) dried fruit, (d) rice.
2 Use some flour to find out the following information:
   (a) How many level teaspoons are there in a level dessertspoon?
   (b) How many level teaspoons are there in a level tablespoon?
   (c) How many level dessertspoons are there in a level tablespoon?
3 Use some water and a measuring jug to find out:
   (a) How many tablespoons of water measure 100 ml.
   (b) How many millilitres of water a cup and a milk bottle hold.

Questions
1 How would you measure the following without using kitchen scales?
   (a) 100 g flour, (b) 50 g sugar, (c) 10 g rice?
2 What jobs need to be done before starting to cook?
3 Describe two ways of weighing food.

Homework
1 Collect *two* recipes that you would like to use. Read through them carefully. Which parts, if any, are difficult to understand? Rewrite the recipes in your own words.
2 Draw the equipment which you use for weighing and measuring in your home.

WASHING UP

Apart from families who own a dishwasher, most people wash up at least twice a day. Hot water and washing-up liquid help to remove food and grease, but stubborn marks need a little extra help from you.
Follow this easy step-by-step guide for success.

1

Scrape food scraps on to paper and throw them away. Fill dirty saucepans with soapy water and leave them to soak.

2

Sort the washing-up into five groups:
1 Glassware
2 Cutlery (knives, forks, and spoons)
3 Cleanest dishes
4 Dirtiest dishes
5 Pans and tins.

3

Fill a washing-up bowl with water, hot enough to put your hand in. Add one squeeze of washing-up liquid to the water. Washing-up liquid removes grease and dried-up food. A scourer removes stubborn stains, and a dishcloth wipes off the dirt and grease.

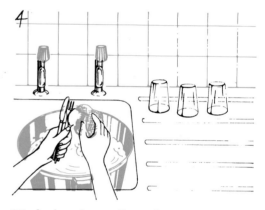

4

Wash the glasses first, then rinse in hot water and drain.
Now wash the cutlery, rinse and drain.

5

First wash the cleaner dishes, then the dirtier ones. Rinse them in hot water, then stack on the draining-board.

6

If the water is very dirty, change it now. Then wash the tins, pots, and saucepans. A scourer may be useful for removing difficult marks.

7

The most hygienic method of drying is to let things dry on their own. If you are in a hurry, dry up with a clean tea-towel, and put the things away.

8

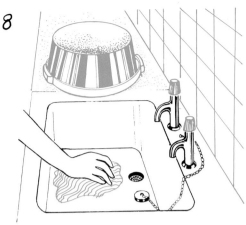

Empty out the dirty water. Wipe down the sink and draining-board and clean the washing-up bowl. Remove any food trapped in the plughole.

9

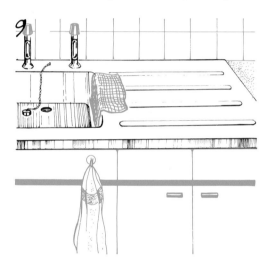

Dry down the draining-board. Wash the tea-towel and dishcloth and leave them to dry. A damp, dirty dishcloth is a breeding ground for bacteria and smells unpleasant.

10

Handy tips
Sharp knives should be washed on their own.
A brush can remove food from graters.
Pastry cutters can be wiped with kitchen paper.
Baking tins can be dried in the oven.

Questions
Describe how you would clean the following pieces of equipment, and list any safety points to be considered:

(a) burnt saucepan   (b) cheese on a grater   (c) food left on a dinner plate   (d) greasy sharp knife

Food is cooked by **heat energy**. There are three methods by which heat can be passed to food: **conduction, convection**, and **radiation.**

Conduction

Heat is **conducted** from molecule to molecule in solid things or liquids. For example, the gas flame heats the base of the saucepan, and the heat is conducted all round the pan. Heat is conducted through food as it is cooked, e.g. heat is conducted through meat when it is roasted.

When choosing cooking pots, it is important to understand about conduction. If a saucepan has a metal handle, then the heat will be conducted along the handle too! Wooden or plastic handles are poor conductors of heat, so they do not get hot. Hot liquids should be stirred with a wooden spoon, not a metal spoon. The metal spoon conducts the heat and gets hot.

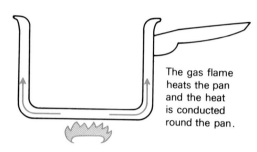

The gas flame heats the pan and the heat is conducted round the pan.

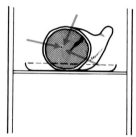

Heat is conducted through food by passing from molecule to molecule.

Convection

Heat travels round liquids and air by a process of **convection currents**.
Hot air and hot liquids rise.
Cold air and cold liquids fall.
Next time you have a bath, notice how the water is colder at the bottom, and hotter at the top of the bath.
Ovens are **heated** by convection currents. **Fridges** are **cooled** by convection currents.
Convection currents pass heat to the food in cooking. Methods of cooking which use convection currents to heat up food are: boiling, deep fat frying, baking in the oven.

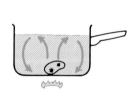

Convection currents in a liquid

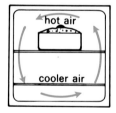

Convection currents in an oven

Radiation

Heat travels from one place to another by rays. The sun, a fire, and a grill on a cooker all give out heat by rays. Food which is grilled or toasted is cooked by **radiant heat.**

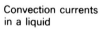

Food is grilled by radiant heat.

A fire heats the surroundings by radiant heat.

Here are some examples of the ways in which heat helps food to cook.

How do grilled sausages cook?

Radiant heat travels to the food.
Heat is conducted through the
sausages and cooks them.

radiant heat

conducted heat

How does a boiled egg cook?

Heat is conducted through the
saucepan and warms the water.
Convection currents carry heat
around the water to the egg.
Heat is conducted through the
egg and cooks it.

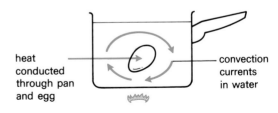

heat conducted through pan and egg

convection currents in water

How does a potato cook in the oven?

Convection currents carry heat
around the oven to the potato.
Heat is conducted through the
potato and cooks it.

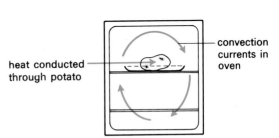

heat conducted through potato

convection currents in oven

How do beefburgers cook in a frying pan?

Heat is conducted through the
frying pan and warms the fat.
The hot fat and hot pan conduct
heat to the beefburgers. Heat is
conducted through the
beefburgers and cooks them.

heat conducted through pan and beefburgers

From each of these three pictures, work out how heat passes to the food and
cooks it.

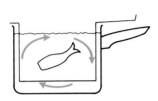 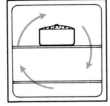 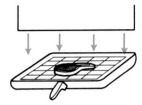

Deep fat fried fish   A cake baked in the oven   A grilled lamb chop

Questions

1 Explain, using examples, what is meant by conduction, convection, and radiation.
2 Why is it important:
   (a) not to use a saucepan with a metal handle?
   (b) not to stir with a metal spoon?

Food is cooked to make it safer and easier to eat. Cooking improves the flavour of some foods, and interesting, tasty dishes can be made. Food can be cooked using hot water, hot fat, or 'dry' heat.

Hot water is used in boiling, stewing, and steaming food.

Hot fat is used for frying and roasting.

'Dry' heat means that the food is cooked by the heat from the oven or grill alone. Baking and grilling use 'dry' heat.

Cooking with water

Water is able to pass heat quickly to food by means of **conduction** and **convection currents**.

Cooking methods which use water:

Boiling Vegetables, meat, pasta, and rice can be cooked in boiling water.

Simmering Not such a vigorous method of cooking as boiling. The liquid bubbles very gently.

Stewing Meat or vegetables can be stewed by simmering gently in hot liquid.

Poaching Fish or eggs can be cooked gently in a little liquid.

Steaming Steam heats the container and cooks food slowly.

A pressure cooker cooks food quickly by increasing the temperature of the liquid above boiling point.

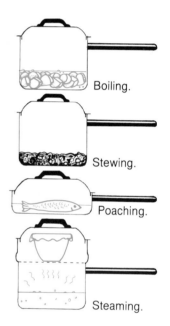

Boiling.

Stewing.

Poaching.

Steaming.

Cooking with fat

Frying Fat is able to cook food at a much higher temperature than water, and so frying is a quick method of cooking.

Shallow frying A low-sided pan is used, with only a little fat. Cooking oil or lard may be used to fry food in.

Dry frying Fatty foods, such as bacon and sausages, can be cooked in their own fat.

Deep fat frying Food is completely surrounded by hot fat in a deep pan, and cooks very quickly.

Food should be dry before frying, as any water will make the fat spit. Many fried foods, e.g. fish, need a protective coating such as egg and breadcrumbs.

Foods to shallow fry:
eggs, fish fingers, beefburgers.

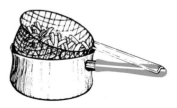

Foods to deep fry:
chips, chicken, fish, Scotch eggs.

Warning: Hot fat can scald, and a pan of fat can catch fire.
Do not let the fat get too hot, and *do* control the heat under the pan.
Never leave frying food unattended in case the fat catches fire.
Keep a damp towel or lid handy to smother the flames.

Roasting Food is roasted in fat in the oven, and basted with the fat to improve the flavour and prevent the food from drying out.
Basting means pouring hot fat over food. Foods which can be roasted include meat, poultry, and vegetables such as potatoes and onions.

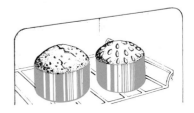

Cooking with 'dry' heat

Baking Baked foods are cooked in the oven. Convection currents carry the heat around the oven into the food.
Grilling Grilling is a quick method of cooking by radiant heat. Foods suitable for grilling include chops, sausages, bacon, and beefburgers. Tough meats cannot be grilled. Tender food such as mushrooms or fish need to be brushed with a little fat.

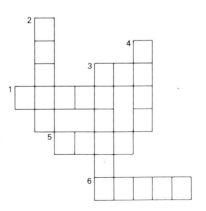

Cooking crossword

Across
1 What food is boiled in.   (5)
3 What food is fried in.   (3)
5 To b_____ potatoes in hot water.   (4)
6 A method for cooking toast and chops.   (5)

Down
2 Boiling water turns into s_____.   (5)
3 A method of cooking using fat.   (6)
4 A gentle way to cook meat in liquid.   (4)

Questions
1 Using examples, describe *three* ways of frying food.
2 Which methods of cooking use (a) hot fat, (b) hot water?
3 Give *three* reasons why food is cooked.
4 Write a sentence about each of the following: stewing, poaching, steaming, roasting, basting.
5 Suggest two ways to cook each of the following foods: potatoes, chicken, sausages, fish, eggs, cooking apples.

Homework
1 Find out about these methods of cooking: pot-roasting, braising, casseroling. Write two sentences about each.
2 List six methods of cooking and suggest two foods which can be cooked by each method. A recipe book may help.

PASTRY

The Romans invented a flour and water paste which was wrapped round meat to be roasted, but was not eaten. Later, fat and milk were added to this mixture to make a pastry similar to today's shortcrust pastry.

Types of pastry

Shortcrust is the most popular pastry, used for sweet and savoury dishes.
Suet pastry is used for steak and kidney pudding and jam roly-poly.
Hot water crust pastry is used for pork pies.
Flaky and rough puff pastry are used to make crispy sausage rolls and pies.
Choux pastry is used for chocolate eclairs.

Ingredients used for pastry

Fat Lard makes pastry short and crisp, and margarine gives colour and flavour. Shortcrust pastry contains less fat than flaky or rough puff pastry and so is a better choice for most dishes.

Flour Plain white flour is most often used for pastry, as self-raising flour makes a crumbly pastry. Wholemeal flour makes a nutty, crumbly pastry, rich in dietary fibre. Good pastry can be made with half white and half wholemeal flour.

Tips for successful pastry-making

1 Read the recipe through to check you have everything you need.

2 Switch on the oven and check the position of the shelves.

3 Collect all the equipment.

4 Work in a cool room with cool work surfaces and equipment.

5 Measure liquids and ingredients accurately.

6 Mix the pastry quickly.

Shortcrust pastry

Proportions: half fat to flour.

Flour Use plain white or wholemeal flour.
Fat Use a mixture of lard and margarine.
Salt is added.
Water must be very cold.

Method: Oven 200°C, 400°F, Gas 6.

Rub the fat into the flour and salt.   Mix to a dough with cold water.   Knead on a floured surface.   Roll out the pastry.

Popular recipes using shortcrust pastry include jam tarts, apple pie, and quiche.

All-in-one shortcrust pastry

This quick way to make shortcrust pastry uses soft margarine. Put the margarine, some flour, and the water into a bowl and cream together with a fork. Work in the remaining flour and knead the dough.

Decorations

Make up 100 g of shortcrust pastry (100 g plain flour, salt, 50 g fat, 1 tbs water). Cover a saucer with some of the pastry and imagine that this is the top of a pie. Invent ways of decorating the pastry. Use any spare pastry to make decorations.

Questions
1 Name four different pastries, and name a dish which can be made from each.
2 Make a list of tips for successful pastry making.
3 Describe how to make shortcrust pastry.

Homework
1 Describe *ten* dishes which can be made from shortcrust pastry.
2 Find out about these different types of pastry:
   suet, hot water crust, flaky, choux, rough puff.
   Make a chart with these headings:
   Type of pastry   How the fat is added   Dishes it can be used for
   Fill in the details for each pastry.

CAKES

Follow these rules before you start to make a cake:
1 Read the recipe through.
2 Prepare the cake tins.
3 Switch on the oven.
4 Weigh the ingredients accurately.
5 Collect all the equipment you need.

The ingredients most commonly used
in cake-making are:

Eggs – size 3 or 4.
Caster sugar is the most popular sweetener.
Flour – white self-raising, plain, or wholemeal.
Butter or **margarine**.

Flavourings such as ginger, mixed spice, vanilla, dried fruit, and nuts can be
added to cakes. **Baking powder** or **bicarbonate of soda** may be added to help
the cake rise, if plain flour is used.

How to test if a cake is cooked

A skewer should
come out clean.

The cake should
be golden brown,
and shrunk from
the tin. The cake
should spring back
when touched.

Tips

Cool a cake on a
wire rack to let
the steam
evaporate.

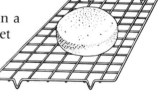

Store the cool
cake in a tin with
a tight-fitting lid.

Cake-making methods

The different methods for making cakes are named after the way the cakes are
prepared. The methods are: **rubbing-in, creaming, melting,** and **whisking.**

Rubbing-in method (Oven 200°C, 400°F, Gas 6)

These cakes contain only half the amount of fat to flour. Do not keep them too
long, because they become dry. The flavourings which can be added include
ginger, mixed spice, and dried fruit. Popular recipes include rock cakes,
raspberry buns, and coconut buns.

Rub fat into flour with
fingertips, until it is like
breadcrumbs.

Add sugar and other
flavourings.

Beat egg with a little
milk, and add to make a
stiff dough.

Creaming method (Oven 190°C, 375°F, Gas 5)

The amount of fat used is usually equal to the amount of flour. It is too messy to try to rub this amount of fat in, so the creaming method is used. Popular recipes using the creaming method include Victoria sandwich, fairy cakes, Christmas cakes, and Eve's pudding.

Cream fat and sugar until fluffy.

Add beaten eggs and beat well. Add any flavourings.

Use a metal spoon and quickly stir in the flour.

There is also an 'all-in-one' method for making cakes. Use soft margarine, and simply put all the ingredients in a bowl and beat the mixture.

Whisking method (Oven 190°C, 375°F, Gas 5)

These cakes usually contain just eggs, sugar and flour. The recipe makes a light sponge which does not keep long. Popular recipes include Swiss roll, sponge sandwiches, and sponge fingers.

Whisk the eggs and sugar until thick and fluffy.

Gently fold in the flour.

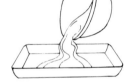

Pour the mixture into a tin.

Melting method (Oven 180°C, 350°F, Gas 4)

Cakes made by this method keep well. Gingerbread is meant to improve with age! Popular recipes include gingerbread and malt loaf.

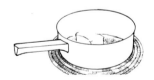

Melt fat and sugar gently in a pan.

Mix flour and other dry ingredients in a bowl.

Add the melted ingredients and mix well.

Questions
1 What steps should be taken when preparing to cook a cake?
2 How can you tell if a cake is cooked?
3 List the four methods of cake-making. Name two cakes made by each method.

Homework
1 Find out and write down detailed recipes for the following cakes: Victoria sandwich, rock cakes, Swiss roll, gingerbread.
2 Collect pictures of cakes and ingredients used in cake-making. Find out which method is used for each cake, and describe your favourite recipe.

Raising agents are added to mixtures to make them rise. Without raising agents, cakes, bread, and scones would all be flat. There are three types of raising agent used in cooking: **air, steam,** and **carbon dioxide gas.**

How does a raising agent work?

Each of the raising agents is a gas. In a hot oven, this gas expands, rises, and pushes up the surrounding mixture.

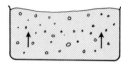 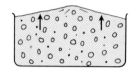 

Bubbles of gas form in the cake, and some rise to the surface.

The bubbles grow larger in the heat of the oven, and push up the cake.

Some gas escapes and some is trapped as the cake cooks.

Experiment

Cover an empty milk bottle with a balloon. Stand the bottle in a saucepan of boiling water, and watch the balloon blow up. Then cool the bottle in cold water, and the balloon should shrink.

Why does this happen?
Air expands on heating. Hot air rises and fills the balloon. On cooling, the gas contracts and sinks.

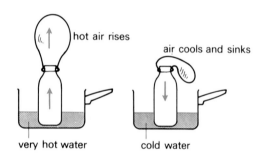

hot air rises

air cools and sinks

very hot water   cold water

Air

Air is used as a raising agent in Swiss roll, meringues, cakes, and other dishes. Air is introduced into mixtures by several methods:

1 Sieving flour
2 Rubbing in fat to flour
3 Beating batters
4 Whisking egg whites
5 Creaming fat and sugar
6 Rolling and folding pastry

To do: Show how much air is introduced into flour by sieving.

Put 100 g flour into a measuring jug. Level it and read the measurement.

Sieve the flour onto some paper, then sieve it back into the jug.

Has the volume increased?
By how much?

Steam

When water is heated to boiling point, the water changes to steam and evaporates. In a very hot oven water in mixtures also evaporates as steam.

As the steam escapes, it pushes up the mixture, leaving it to set. Dishes such as Yorkshire pudding, eclairs and flaky pastry use steam as their raising agent and should be cooked in a hot oven.

Carbon dioxide

There are two ways to produce carbon dioxide gas in a mixture:
1 Use chemicals such as bicarbonate of soda or baking powder.
2 Allow yeast to grow and ferment.

Chemical raising agents

When **bicarbonate of soda** or **baking powder** is mixed with water and heated, **carbon dioxide gas** is given off.

Baking powder is used to raise rich cakes and scones.
Bicarbonate of soda is used in gingerbread and chocolate cake.
Self-raising flour has chemicals added to it, which include bicarbonate of soda. This flour helps cakes like Victoria sandwich to rise.

An experiment to show how chemical raising agents work

Put half a level teaspoon of bicarbonate of soda into test tube A, and half a level teaspoon of baking powder into test tube B. Add 3 cm of hot water to each test tube. Shake and cover the test tubes with balloons. As each mixture bubbles, carbon dioxide gas is given off and fills the balloon. This bubbling is called **effervescence**. When the effervescence stops, taste the liquids.

The liquid from the bicarbonate of soda will taste soapy, since it contains **washing soda**. Baking powder does not have this unpleasant taste.

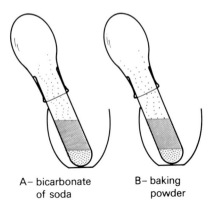

A– bicarbonate of soda   B– baking powder

Make some fizzy orange

Fill a glass with strong orange squash. Stir in half a teaspoon of bicarbonate of soda and drink quickly.

When bicarbonate of soda is mixed with water, it bubbles and gives off carbon dioxide gas, which is trapped in the water for a short time.

Questions
1 List *three* raising agents and show how each is introduced into flour mixtures.
2 State *four* ways in which air is added to mixtures.
3 Self-raising flour gives off carbon dioxide gas when wet and warm. Decide whether to use self-raising or plain flour in the following dishes: gravy, shortcrust pastry, fairy cakes, Swiss roll.

Yeast

Yeast is a single-celled plant fungus. These cells can only be seen under the microscope. Yeast needs **food, warmth**, and **liquid** to grow and ferment. During fermentation carbon dioxide gas is produced.

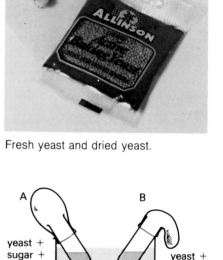
Fresh yeast and dried yeast.

Compare fresh and dried yeast

Smell and feel the fresh yeast. Mix some fresh yeast with a little water and smear this on to a glass slide. Use a microscope to look at the yeast cells. Make up a little of the dried yeast as instructed on the packet. Examine it. Describe and compare the two types of yeast.

Experiment to show that yeast needs food to ferment

Equipment

2 test tubes	10 g fresh yeast
2 balloons	pinch sugar
2 labels	small bowl

1 Label the test tubes A and B.
2 Into A put 5 g yeast, a pinch of sugar and 1 cm of warm water.
3 Into B place 5 g yeast and 1 cm of warm water.
4 Cover each test tube with a balloon and stand in a bowl of warm water for twenty minutes.

What should happen?
The balloon on test tube A gradually blows up, because the yeast feeds from the sugar and produces carbon dioxide gas.
The balloon on test tube B remains flat, because the yeast has no food.

How bread is made

200 g plain flour	15 g fresh yeast
25 g margarine	1 level tsp sugar
1 level tsp salt	150 ml water

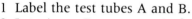

 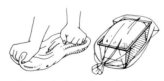 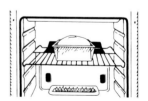

Mix yeast, sugar, and water. Rub fat into flour and salt, then add the yeast liquid and mix the dough.

Knead the dough. Put into a tin and leave to prove (rise) inside a greased plastic bag, till it has doubled in size.

Bake in a very hot oven, 220°C, 425°F, Gas 7, for 30 minutes.

How does the yeast help the bread to rise?

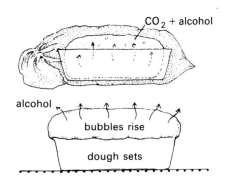

Proving: The yeast uses the flour and sugar for food and ferments, producing carbon dioxide gas and alcohol. The dough increases in size and bubbles can be seen in the dough.

Baking: Carbon dioxide gas expands and pushes up the dough. The yeast is killed, the alcohol escapes, and the dough sets.

Make some ginger beer

Ingredients
Juice and rind of 1 lemon
450 g granulated sugar
25 g dried ground ginger
15 g fresh yeast
1 slice toast
2.3 litres boiling water
2.3 litres cold water

Method
1 Put the lemon rind, ginger, and sugar in a large bowl, and pour over the boiling water. Then add the cold water and leave to cool.
2 Spread the yeast on the toast and float on the mixture.
3 Cover with a clean tea towel and leave for 24 hours.
4 Remove the scum and pour the clear liquid into bottles.
5 Seal with screwtops or corks tied down with wire.
6 Leave for three days in a cool place and drink within three days.

Quiz

Find the hidden word in the green box.
1 _____ can be sieved or whisked into mixtures. (3)
2 Bicarbonate of soda is a ch_____ added to help mixtures rise. (8)
3 Y_____ ferments and is used to make bread. (5)
4 Liquids evaporate into s_____, as in Yorkshire pudding. (5)

Homework
Collect some pictures of different bread and yeast mixtures. Find out and describe how yeast is used to make different cakes, buns, and breads.

FURTHER WORK

Experiment to show the effect of washing-up liquid on grease

Take two glasses. Into glass A put water and into glass B put water plus a squirt of washing-up liquid. Add 15 ml of cooking oil to glass A. Stir, then allow it to settle and notice how the oil floats to the top. Add 15 ml of cooking oil to glass B. Stir vigorously. If there is enough washing-up liquid present, the oil should disappear.

Why does this happen?
The detergent molecules in the washing-up liquid surround the oil drops. The oil cannot float on top of the water, because it is broken into small droplets which spread throughout the water.

What happens when you wash up?

The dirty dishes are placed in a bowl of hot water and the washing-up liquid is added. The detergent molecules in the washing-up liquid attach themselves to the dirt and grease on the crockery. The dirt and grease can then float away or be rubbed off into the water.

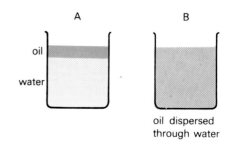

A   B

oil

water

oil dispersed
through water

● oil droplets
○ detergent molecules

Oil is broken into droplets
and surrounded by detergent.

Compare homemade pastry with packet-mix shortcrust and frozen shortcrust

Buy (1) a packet mix of shortcrust pastry
(2) some frozen shortcrust pastry
Prepare (3) some homemade shortcrust pastry using 100 g flour. (See p. 106.)

Make up the three batches of shortcrust pastry into three sets of jam tarts and bake them. When the tarts are baked and cool, form a tasting panel and ask the panel to describe which pastry they liked the best and why.

Work out the cost of the bought pastry compared with the homemade pastry. Write a report comparing the different pastries. Describe how long each took to prepare, how much each cost, and the quality of the cooked pastry. What are the good and bad points about using each pastry?

Recipes may show three different oven temperatures. New electric ovens have Celsius temperature measurements (°C), whereas older electric ovens still measure using the Fahrenheit scale (°F). Gas ovens have numbers for their thermostat settings.

Oven temperatures

Type of food to be cooked	Gas setting	Electrical oven temperature		
		°C	°F	
plate warming, rich cakes, egg custard	$\frac{1}{4}$–2	110–150	225–300	cool
plain cakes, fish	3–4	160–180	325–350	moderate
shortcrust pastry, small cakes, Swiss roll	5–6	190–200	375–400	fairly hot
scones, bread, Yorkshire pudding	7–8	220–230	425–450	hot
browning food quickly	9	240	475	very hot

Glossary

Here are some simple cookery terms which you may find in recipes:

to beat: to mix ingredients by beating quickly with a spoon.
to blend: to add liquid to a powder to make a smooth paste.
to cream: to mix fat and sugar until they are white and fluffy.
to fold: to add one ingredient to another gently, e.g. flour to whisked eggs.
to garnish: to decorate food to make it look more attractive.
to glaze: to brush uncooked dishes with beaten egg or milk to improve their appearance when cooked.
to grease: to cover a baking tin with fat, either by brushing with a little oil, or using margarine paper. This stops food from sticking once it is cooked.
to liquidize: to change solid food into a liquid, by using a machine called a liquidizer, which has sharp cutting blades to chop up food.
to rub in: to mix fat lightly into flour using the fingertips.
to season: to add flavour to food by using salt, pepper, herbs, and spices.
to simmer: to cook a liquid over a low heat, just below boiling point.
to whisk: to beat air into ingredients, e.g. egg whites.

Abbreviations used in recipes: g – gram   ml – millilitre   SR – self-raising

Answers to the quiz on p. 74

1 false	5 false	9 false	13 false
2 true	6 true	10 false	14 false
3 true	7 false	11 false	
4 true	8 false (rare steaks)	12 false	

Score: 12 and over: well done! 10–12: quite good; below 10: a poor result

6. RECIPES

RECIPES

Most of the recipes chosen for this book can be prepared and cooked in less than an hour, so they could be made during a home economics lesson. The recipes use inexpensive ingredients and test a range of skills

Parts of the recipes can be used to prepare other dishes. For example, the mince mixture of spaghetti bolognese can be served on its own, or used for shepherd's pie. The all-in-one sauce and tomato sauce can be served with meat, fish fingers, or pasta.

Cheesy-tomato toasted topping (serves 2)

Ingredients

2 slices of bread	50 g cheese		
25 g margarine	2 eggs		
salt and pepper	1 tomato		

Equipment

serrated knife	wooden spoon
small bowl	chopping board
fork	tablespoon
small saucepan	grater
pastry brush	plate

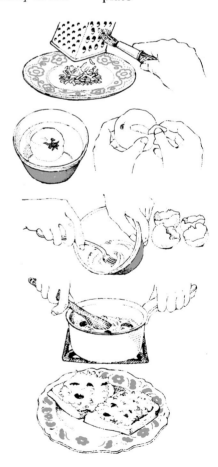

Method

1 Grate the cheese on to the plate using a grater. Brush off the remaining cheese with a pastry brush.

2 Put the tomato in boiling water for two minutes, until the skin bursts. Peel off the skin, and slice the tomato on a chopping board, using a serrated knife. (If the tomato is not peeled, pieces of skin float off into the cooking mixture.)

3 Break two eggs in a bowl. Add some salt and pepper and beat the mixture with a fork. Add the sliced tomato and turn on the grill.

4 Put the margarine into the saucepan, and place the saucepan over a low heat. Pour the egg mixture into the pan and cook slowly, stirring with a wooden spoon so that the egg does not stick to the pan. The eggs are ready when they are set, but still moist. Stir in the grated cheese.

5 Place the slices of bread under the hot grill, and cook until they are golden brown on both sides.

6 Pile the cheesy-tomato topping on to the toast and eat it immediately.

This topping can be served hot or cold, with toast or sandwiches.

Crunchy spicy apple (serves 4)

Ingredients

1 kilo cooking apples
50 g sugar
½ level teaspoon mixed spice
1 tablespoon golden syrup
10 g rice crispies
10 g margarine

Equipment

vegetable knife or potato peeler
chopping board
large saucepan and lid
wooden spoon
tablespoon
small saucepan
serving dish

Method

1 Peel the skin from the apples, using a vegetable knife or potato peeler. Use the knife to cut the apple into quarters and remove the cores.
2 Put the apple in a large saucepan with three tablespoons of water. Cover with a tightly fitting lid, and cook gently for 5–10 minutes until the apple is soft and fluffy.
3 Stir in the sugar and spice and pile the apple into the serving dish.
4 Heat a tablespoon in hot water, then measure out a spoonful of syrup into a small saucepan. Add the margarine and stir over a low heat until the margarine has melted.
5 Toss in the crispies, using a tablespoon. When all the crispies are coated with the mixture, spoon this topping on to the apple.

Custard

Ingredients

500 ml milk
2 rounded tablespoons
    custard powder
1 rounded tablespoon sugar

Equipment

small saucepan
wooden spoon
tablespoon
mixing bowl
serving jug

Method

1 Pour most of the milk into a saucepan and place over the heat to boil.
2 Mix the custard powder into a smooth paste using the remaining milk. Mix in a mixing bowl, using a wooden spoon.
3 Pour the boiling milk on to the mixture, then return the mixture to the pan and bring back to the boil, stirring with a wooden spoon.
4 Remove the saucepan from the heat and add the sugar. Serve in a jug.

Tomato soup (serves 3–4)

Delicious, yet simple soups can be made from all sorts of vegetables: for example, mushrooms, onions, leeks, and potatoes. Soups can take about ten minutes to cook if the ingredients are finely chopped – this may be quicker than some dried soup mixes! For tomato soup you need:

Ingredients	Equipment
1 medium tin of tomatoes (400 g)	sieve
1 small onion	cook's knife
1 carrot	chopping board
1 rasher of bacon	potato peeler
1 level tablespoon flour	large saucepan
2 tablespoons oil	with lid
300 ml water	wooden spoon
1 chicken stock cube	measuring jug
salt, pepper, sugar,	teaspoon
nutmeg (pinch of each)	small bowl
1 dessertspoon cornflour (if needed)	scissors

Method

1 Open the tin of tomatoes and liquidize or strain them through a sieve to form a thick juice.

2 Chop the bacon, leaving on the rind, using either a cook's knife or scissors. Peel and chop the onion using a cook's knife. Scrape the carrot with a potato peeler or knife, then chop the carrot into dice using a cook's knife.

3 Heat the oil in the saucepan. Add the bacon, onion, and carrot and fry gently for three minutes, stirring with a wooden spoon. Stir in the flour and add the tomato juice, water, salt, pepper, sugar, and nutmeg. Stir the mixture until it boils.

4 Turn down the heat, put the lid on the pan, and simmer for 15 minutes.

This soup can be served with pieces of vegetables, or sieved or liquidized to make a smooth soup.

Use a teaspoon to taste the soup, adding more salt or pepper if necessary. If the soup needs to be thickened, blend a level dessertspoon of cornflour with water, in a small bowl, and add a little to the soup. Heat the soup, and stir until it thickens. Add enough cornflour mixture to thicken the soup to your liking.

Spaghetti bolognese (serves 2)

Ingredients
200 g mince
1 onion
50 g mushrooms
3 tablespoons tomato ketchup
salt, pepper, mixed herbs (pinch of each)
50 g spaghetti
50 g grated Cheddar or Parmesan cheese

Equipment
2 large saucepans, one with lid
wooden spoon
chopping board
cook's knife
serrated knife
colander
grater
serving dish

Method

1 Fry the mince gently in a large saucepan without using extra fat. Stir with a wooden spoon until the meat begins to turn brown.
2 Peel and chop the onion finely using a cook's knife. Wash the mushrooms under running water. Remove any damaged parts, then slice, using a serrated or cook's knife.
3 Add the onion and mushrooms to the mince and fry for 5 more minutes.
4 Stir in the tomato ketchup, salt, pepper, and mixed herbs. Cover the pan with a lid and cook gently for 15 minutes. Put the serving dish to warm in a low oven or warming drawer.

5 While the mince is cooking, half fill a saucepan with boiling water and add one level teaspoon of salt.
6 Dip one end of the spaghetti into the water. Wait until it softens, then wind the spaghetti round in the water until it is completely covered by water. Boil quickly for 10 minutes with the lid off, until the spaghetti is tender.

7 The spaghetti needs draining. *Boiling water can scald*, so carry the saucepan to the sink. Carefully drain off the water by pouring the contents of the saucepan through a colander which is held over the sink.
8 Place the spaghetti on a warm serving dish, pour the meat sauce over it, and sprinkle grated cheese on top of the meat.

Fisherman's pie (serves 2)

Ingredients
500 g potatoes
25 g margarine
salt, pepper
100 ml milk
small tin of sweetcorn
300 g inexpensive fish (coley, whiting)

Sauce
25 g flour
25 g margarine
300 ml milk
50 g grated cheese

Equipment
large saucepan and lid
metal plate
potato peeler
cook's knife
palette knife
small saucepan
wooden spoon
grater
fork
tablespoon
sieve
potato masher
serving dish

Method

1 Half-fill a saucepan with boiling salted water. Scrub then peel the potatoes, using a potato peeler. Cut them into quarters, using a cook's knife. Place in the boiling water and cook for 15–20 minutes until soft. Test for softness by pushing a fork into the potato.

2 While the potatoes are cooking, cover the saucepan with a metal plate. Place the fish on the plate with a knob of margarine. Cover the plate with the saucepan lid and steam the fish for 10 minutes. Warm a serving dish.

3 Prepare an all-in-one sauce: place the milk, flour, and margarine in a saucepan and heat this mixture, stirring with a wooden spoon. When the mixture thickens, add salt, pepper, and grated cheese.

4 Flake the cooked fish by mashing it with a fork. Remove any skin or bones. Add the fish and sweetcorn to the sauce and pour this mixture into the serving dish. Turn on the grill.

5 When the potatoes are soft, drain in a sieve, return to the pan, and mash with a fork or potato masher. Add 100 ml of milk, 25 g margarine and salt and pepper. Beat with a wooden spoon until smooth and creamy.

6 Pile the potato on top of the fish. Level the surface with a knife and make a pattern with a fork. Grill the dish until the potato turns golden brown.

Kebabs with savoury rice and tomato sauce (serves 2)

Order of work: cook rice, prepare and cook kebabs, prepare sauce.

Kebabs

Ingredients
2 rashers of streaky bacon
4 button mushrooms
1 small tomato
1 small onion
2 sausages
a little cooking oil

Equipment
scissors
serrated and cook's knife
2 skewers
pastry brush
fork
serving dish

Method

1 Turn the grill to a medium heat, to warm up.
2 Take the rind off the bacon, cut each rasher in half and roll into bacon rolls.
3 Cut each sausage in half or twist into two small sausages.
4 Peel the onion and cut into quarters. Wash the tomato and cut into quarters. Wash and dry the mushrooms.
5 Use two skewers. Thread each skewer with bacon, onion, sausage, tomato, mushroom, and so on until each skewer is full. Brush the food with oil and arrange the skewers on the grill pan.
6 Grill for 5 minutes, then turn the skewers over and grill the food for a further 5 minutes. Warm a serving dish.

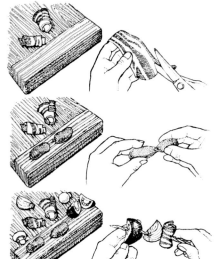

Savoury rice

Ingredients
100 g long grain rice
1 small packet of frozen mixed vegetables (about 100 g)
salt and pepper

Equipment
large saucepan
teaspoon
sieve

Method

1 Half-fill a large saucepan with boiling water.
2 Add a level teaspoon of salt and return the pan to the heat for the water to boil again.
3 Add the rice and cook the rice in the water for $11\frac{1}{2}$ minutes *exactly*, without the lid on.
4 Strain the rice through a sieve and return it to the saucepan, adding the mixed vegetables. Warm gently for two minutes, adding some pepper and salt to taste.

Tomato sauce

Ingredients
1 small tin of tomatoes
salt, pepper, sugar, mixed herbs (pinch of each)
1 level tablespoon cornflour

Equipment
small saucepan
wooden spoon

Method

1 Sieve or liquidize the tomatoes to make a smooth juice.
2 Place all the ingredients in a saucepan. Heat, stirring all the time using a wooden spoon, until the mixture thickens. Taste and add more seasoning if necessary.
3 Serve the kebabs on a bed of savoury rice and pour the tomato sauce over the top. 121

Quick pizza (serves 2)

Ingredients
100 g SR flour
25 g margarine
pinch of salt
water to mix

Topping
50 g grated cheese
1 rasher of bacon
1 tomato
½ onion
mixed herbs
olives (optional)

Equipment
baking tray   serrated knife
mixing bowl   chopping board
tablespoon   grater
palette knife   teaspoon
small bowl   scissors
cook's knife

Method

1 Turn on the oven to 200°C/ 400°F/ Gas 6. Grease a baking tray with cooking oil or margarine paper.

2 Sieve the flour and salt into a mixing bowl. Rub in the margarine with the fingertips, until the mixture looks like breadcrumbs. Add two tablespoons of cold water and work into the mixture, using a palette knife. When the mixture begins to stick together, form the dough into a ball using the hands.

3 Put a little flour on the work surface and pat out the dough into a circle about 14 cm in diameter. Place on the baking tray.

4 Slice the onion and tomato using a serrated or cook's knife. Place on top of the dough, then cover with grated cheese and mixed herbs. Take the rind off the bacon, using a pair of scissors. Cut the bacon lengthways and arrange it in a cross on top of the pizza. Decorate with olives or leave plain.

5 Bake the pizza for 20–30 minutes, until the dough is thoroughly cooked. Test the dough by lifting it with a knife to see if the centre is dry and cooked.

6 Serve the pizza hot or cold.

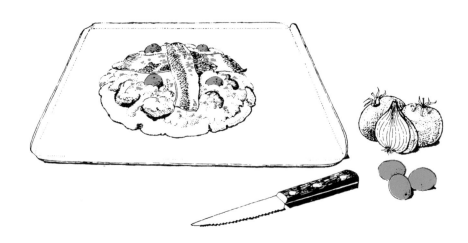

Chicken casserole (serves 2)

Ingredients
2 chicken pieces (legs or wings)
1 rasher of bacon
2 tablespoons oil
1 carrot
1 level dessertspoon flour
2 tablespoons tomato ketchup
1 chicken stock cube
salt, pepper, mixed herbs (pinch of each)

Equipment
ovenproof dish   scissors
baking tray   potato peeler
large saucepan   tablespoon
wooden spoon   measuring jug
fork   cook's knife
chopping board

Method

1 Turn on the oven to 190°C/375°F/Gas 5. Place an ovenproof dish, with a lid on, on a baking tray.

2 Wash and clean the chicken, removing any feathers. Heat the oil in a large saucepan, and fry both chicken portions, turning over after 5 minutes to fry the other side for 5 minutes.

3 Meanwhile, remove the bacon rind and chop the bacon. Scrape the carrot and cut into dice. Peel and chop the onion.

4 Remove the chicken portions and place in the dish in the oven.

5 Fry the bacon, onion, and carrot in the saucepan for 2 minutes, stirring with a wooden spoon.

6 Add the flour to the saucepan, stir and cook for a further minute.

7 Mix together the stock cube, tomato ketchup, salt, pepper, herbs, and 150 ml of water in a measuring jug, then pour this mixture into the saucepan.

8 Heat this sauce, stirring with a wooden spoon until the mixture boils and thickens.

9 Use oven gloves to remove the dish from the oven. Pour the sauce over the chicken. Cover the dish with the lid, return to the oven and cook for one hour, or until the chicken is tender.

Baked potatoes

4 small potatoes
25 g butter or margarine

Scrub the potatoes clean. With a knife, cut a cross on the potato skin, to prevent the potato from bursting. Bake the potatoes on the top shelf of the oven for one hour, or until they are soft. Place a knob of butter on each potato when they are ready to serve.

Salads

Lots of different salad vegetables can be used to make a salad. The choice depends upon the time of year, and what is in the shops. Try experimenting with fruits and nuts or raw root vegetables in salads.

Vegetables should always be washed carefully under running water to remove dirt and insects, then dried with a clean tea-towel. Use a stainless steel vegetable knife to prepare most salad vegetables.

Here are ways to prepare different vegetables:

Lettuce Wash the leaves separately, then pat dry with a tea-towel. Either tear the leaves into mouth-size pieces or serve the leaves whole.

Mustard and cress Snip off the top part of stems and leaves using scissors. Wash well to remove any seeds or soil.

Spring onions Trim off the root end of the onion, using a knife, and remove any damaged outer skin and leaves. Chop or serve whole.

Radishes Clean carefully and remove roots and leaves. Leave whole or slice into rings.

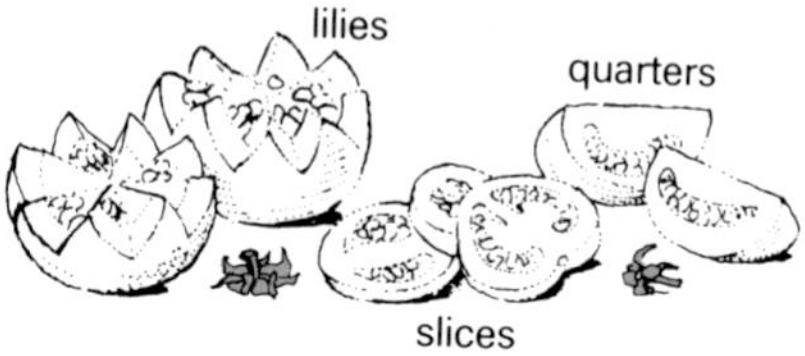

Tomatoes These can be sliced thinly or cut into wedges, using a serrated knife. Tomato lilies can be made by cutting zig-zag around the middle of the tomato.

Celery Scrub each stick well to remove any soil. Slice, chop or serve whole.

Cucumber Wash, then slice finely with a serrated knife.

Tossed salad

A selection of vegetables can be served in a bowl and tossed in French dressing, using a tablespoon and fork.

French dressing

Ingredients
2 tablespoons oil
1 tablespoon wine vinegar
salt, pepper, sugar, mustard powder

Equipment
tablespoon
teaspoon
jam jar and lid

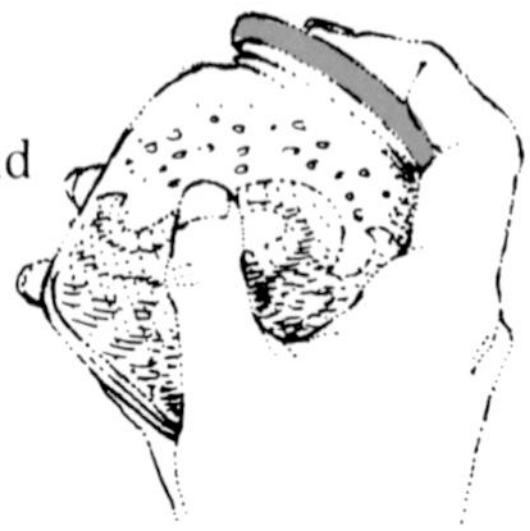

Method
1 Use a jam jar with a tight-fitting lid.
2 Place the oil and vinegar in the jar and add a pinch of each of the seasonings. Shake the jar until the mixture thickens.

Fresh fruit salad (serves 2–4)

Ingredients
1 apple
1 banana
1 orange
a few grapes
2 glacé cherries
½ lemon
10 g caster sugar

Equipment
lemon squeezer
tablespoon
mixing bowl
serrated knife
chopping board
serving dish

Any fresh fruit can be used, e.g. strawberries, cherries, peaches, pears.

Method

1 Squeeze the juice of the lemon and stir in the caster sugar. Place the mixture in a mixing bowl.

2 Prepare the fruit:
Peel and slice the banana and toss in the lemon juice mixture.
Wash, quarter and core the apple. Chop into small pieces and toss in the lemon juice mixture.
Cut the rind off the orange, and divide the flesh into segments. Add to the other fruit.
Wash and halve the grapes, and remove pips.

3 Toss all the fruit together and arrange in a serving dish. Decorate with halved cherries and serve with cream, yoghurt, or custard.

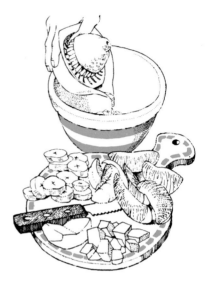

Chocolate crispies

Ingredients
25 g sugar
25 g margarine
2 heaped teaspoons cocoa
1 tablespoon golden syrup
25 g cornflakes

Equipment
tablespoon
small saucepan
wooden spoon
dessertspoon
paper cake cases
teaspoon

Method

1 Put margarine and sugar into the saucepan. Add the golden syrup (warm the tablespoon in hot water first).

2 Put the pan over a gentle heat and slowly melt the ingredients, stirring with a wooden spoon. Add the cocoa.

3 Remove the pan from the heat and toss in the cornflakes, using a tablespoon. When the cornflakes are thoroughly coated, spoon dessertspoons of the mixture into cake cases and leave to set.

Lemon meringue (serves 2–3)

Ingredients

1 lemon
2 eggs
75 g caster sugar
1 level tablespoon cornflour
150 ml water
2 glacé cherries

Equipment

ovenproof dish
grater
pastry brush
lemon squeezer
small saucepan
wooden spoon
measuring jug

2 small bowls
mixing bowl
knife
fork
rotary whisk
chopping board

Method

1 Grease a small ovenproof dish and turn on the oven to 180°C/350°F/Gas 4.
2 Wash the lemon and gently grate the rind into fine pieces. Only the yellow rind (*zest*) should be used, not the bitter white pith. Brush off the zest, using a pastry brush.
3 Squeeze out the lemon juice using a lemon squeezer.
4 Put the lemon juice, zest, 25 g of the sugar, the cornflour and water into a small saucepan. Using a wooden spoon, stir the mixture over the heat until it clears and thickens.
5 Leave this mixture to cool.
6 Separate the eggs into whites and yolks (see p. 40).
7 When the lemon mixture has cooled slightly, beat in the two egg yolks, and pour the mixture into the dish.
8 Whisk the egg whites until they are stiff. Use a rotary whisk, electric whisk, or fork. Whisk in 50 g of sugar, and pile the meringue on top of the lemon mixture.
9 Decorate with the glacé cherries. Bake in the oven for about 20 minutes until the meringue is crisp.

Flapjacks

Ingredients

100 g rolled oats
25 g margarine
1 tablespoon golden syrup
2 heaped teaspoons sugar
25 g sultanas

Equipment

metal plate
small saucepan
wooden spoon
knife

Method

1 Grease a metal plate. Turn on the oven to 180°C/350°F/Gas 4.
2 Gently melt the margarine, syrup, and sugar over a low heat, stirring with a wooden spoon.
3 Remove the saucepan from the heat, and stir in the rolled oats and sultanas.
4 Tip the mixture on to the metal plate and flatten with a knife.
5 Bake in the oven for 30 minutes, then cool for several minutes, before cutting the flapjacks into eight pieces.

Chocolate mousse (serves 2)

Ingredients
50 g plain chocolate
2 eggs (size 4)

Equipment
small saucepan
3 small bowls
mixing bowl
teaspoon

knife
tablespoon
fork
2 serving dishes

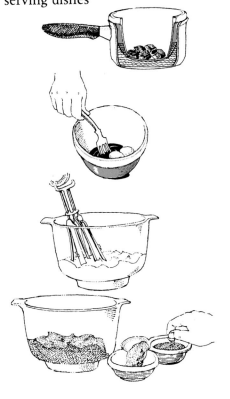

Method
1 Half fill a small saucepan with hot water and fit a small bowl into the saucepan. Melt the chocolate in the bowl over the hot water. Do not allow any water to get into the chocolate.
2 Separate the yolks of the eggs from the whites, using separate bowls for each egg white in case the yolks break. See p. 40 for how to do this.
3 Remove the bowl of melted chocolate from the pan. Beat the yolks into the melted chocolate using a fork.
4 Tip the whites into the mixing bowl. Whisk the egg whites until they are stiff, using a clean rotary whisk, electric whisk or fork. The stiff whites should stick to the sides of the bowl.
5 Fold the chocolate mixture gently into the whisked egg whites, using a tablespoon. This should take no longer than one minute.
6 Spoon the mixture into two small serving dishes and chill in the fridge for half an hour to set the chocolate.

Orange and cinnamon biscuits

Ingredients
100 g margarine
50 g caster sugar
100 g SR flour
zest of an orange
$\frac{1}{2}$ level teaspoon cinnamon

Equipment
baking tray
sieve
mixing bowl
grater
pastry brush
wooden spoon
palette knife
cooling rack
plate

Method
1 Turn on the oven to 190°C/375°F/Gas 5. Grease a baking tray.
2 Sieve the flour and cinnamon on to a plate and add the zest of the orange (see p. 126).
3 Cream the margarine and sugar in a mixing bowl, using a wooden spoon. Add the flour mixture and form into a dough, using firstly the wooden spoon then the hands. Roll the mixture into 18–20 small balls and space them out on a baking tray.
4 Bake for 15–20 minutes, then take the tray out of the oven, using an oven glove, and allow the biscuits to cool for two minutes. Using a palette knife, lift the biscuits on to a cooling rack.